SELECTED WORKS OF MODERN CHINESE LEARNING

THE CHINESE SYSTEM OF PUBLIC EDUCATION

Ping Wen Kuo

商務印書館
SINCE1897 The Commercial Press

2014 • BEIJING

First Edition 2014

ISBN 978-7-100-10002-1

Published by
The Commercial Press
36 Wangfujing Road, Beijing 100710, China
www.cp.com.cn

Ping Wen Kuo

(1880—1969)

Editorial Note

One hundred years ago, Zhang Zhidong tried to advocate Chinese learning by saying: "The course of a nation, be it bright or gloomy, the pool of talents, be it large or small, are about governance on the surface, and about learning at the root." At that time, the imperialist powers cast menacing eyes on our country, and the domestic situation was deteriorating. The quick infiltration of Western learning made the long-standing Chinese tradition come under heavy challenge. In those days, Chinese learning and Western learning stood side by side. Literature, history and philosophy split up, while many new branches of learning such as economics, politics and sociology were flourishing, which made many Chinese dazed. However, there appeared a vital and vigorous learning climate out of the confusing situation. It was at this critical moment that modern Chinese scholarship made the transition—by exchanging views, basing on profound contemplation and even with confrontation of idea and clash of views, the scholarship made continuous progress, bringing up a large number of persons of academic distinction and creating numerous innovative works. Changes in scholarship and in general modes of thinking made transition in all aspects of the society possible, thus laying a solid foundation for revitalizing China.

It's over a century since the journey of modern Chinese learning started, during which various schools of thought stood in great numbers, causing heated discussions. The journey sees schools of thought as well as relevant arguments rising and falling, waxing and waning instantly, leaving complicated puzzles to followers. By studying and reviewing the selected works, one may gain new insights into that journey; and it is the editor's sincere hope that readers would ponder over the future by recalling the past. That's why we have compiled "Selected Works of Modern Chinese Learning". The effort includes masterpieces of celebrated scholars from diverse fields of study and different schools of thought. By tracing back to the source and searching for the basis of modern Chinese learning, we wish to present the dynamics between thought and time.

The series of "Selected Works of Modern Chinese Learning" includes works (both in Chinese and in foreign languages) of scholars from China—mainland, Hong Kong, Macau, and Taiwan—and from overseas. These works are mostly on humanities and cover all fields of subjects, such as literary theory, linguistics, history, philosophy, politics, economics, jurisprudence, sociology, to name a few.

It has been a long-cherished wish of the Commercial Press to compile a series of "Selected Works of Modern Chinese Learning". Since its foundation in 1897, the Commercial Press has been privileged to have published numerous pioneering works and masterpieces of modern Chinese learning under the motto of "promoting education and enlightening people". The press has participated in and witnessed the establishment and development of modern Chinese learning. The series of "Selected Works of Modern Chinese Learning" is fruit of an effort to relay the editorial legacy and the cultural propositions of our senior generations. This series, sponsored by National Publication Foundation, would not be possible if there were no careful planning of the press itself. Neither would it be possible without extensive collaboration among talents of the academic circle. It is our deeply cherished hope that titles of this series will keep their place on the bookshelves even after a long time. Moreover, we wish that this series and "Chinese Translations of World Classics" will become double jade in Chinese publishing history as well as in the history of the Commercial Press itself. With such great aspirations in mind, fearing that it is beyond our ability to realize them, we cordially invite both scholars and readers to extend your assistance.

Editorial Department of the Commercial Press

December 2010

PREFACE

The awakened interest in the new educational era in China has brought into existence, within the last few years, several books in English dealing specifically with the subject of Chinese education. Among these are "The Education of Women in China," by Margaret E. Burton; "The Educational System of China as Recently Reconstructed," by Henry Edwin King; and "Chinese Education From the Western Viewpoint," by Yen Sun Ho. Each of these timely works throws some light upon one or another of the many phases of Chinese education, and hence has a place in the literature of the subject. There is still, however, a great demand for a work which will present a connected account of the Chinese Public Educational System in its long process of development, giving a perspective view of the rise and fall of the ancient and traditional systems of education under successive dynasties, as well as a picture of the modern educational system as it is reorganized under the new republic. The present study is an attempt to fill this want, and, so far as the knowledge of the author goes, it represents the first serious attempt to disentangle the complicated history of Chinese education for the English-speaking public.

In dealing with a subject of this character, the question of selection among the materials available and that of proportion among the parts have been difficult to solve. In spite of the care taken, it will doubtless be found that many things have been omitted which were worthy in every way of a place with those which have been mentioned, and that some phases summarily dealt with might well have been elaborated. In spite of these limitations, I trust that this general sketch of the development of the Chinese Public Educational System may not only be useful to those who are in any way interested in Chinese education, but may also light the way for future research.

The main portion of the data for this study is derived from two general sources. The facts relating to the ancient and traditional system of education are secured from the authoritative encyclopedia by Ma-tuan-lin, entitled "Wen Hsien T'ung K'ao," from the supplement to the same work, and from Biot's work in French, entitled "Essai sur l'Histoire de l'Instruction Publique en Chine." Those relating to modern education are obtained from Chinese educational laws, reports of the Ministry of Education and other educational bodies, and the current numbers of the various educational periodicals, both official and private. Other sources of information are listed in the Bibliography.

I wish to express my thanks to Professors Farrington, Monroe, and Hillegas, of Teachers College, Professor Hirth, of Columbia University, and Dr. Sailer, of the Presbyterian Board of Foreign Missions, as well as to my colleagues Messrs. Yu and Chen for reading my manuscript. My thanks are especially due to the two professors in charge of my major studies, Dr. Strayer and Dr. Farrington, who have taken a deep interest in my work from the beginning to the end.

P. W. Kuo.

New York City,
June 1, 1914

CONTENTS

CHAPTER IV

Transition from Traditional to Modern Education. (A.D. 1842-1905)

CHAPTER V

The Construction of a Modern Educational System (1905–1911)

CHAPTER VI

Reorganization of Education under the Republic

CHAPTER VII

Present-Day Educational Problems of National Importance

CHAPTER VIII

Summary and Conclusions

INTRODUCTION

The intellectual classes among Oriental peoples are keenly conscious of the need of the Orient for Western learning. There is a corresponding need, not so keenly felt however, of a knowledge of Eastern learning and of Eastern aspirations and accomplishment on the part of the Western world. This volume by Dr. Kuo portrays the recent efforts of the largest and in many respects the greatest of Oriental peoples to obtain such a familiarity with Western learning. At the same time it places in a clear light the stages in the long evolution of the native culture and of the educational system of the Chinese. In doing this the author has made a contribution of great importance to the Western knowledge of Eastern conditions.

Sympathetic Western observers who have been long in contact with the Chinese give as their impression that, while there are differences between these people and the Occidentals in point of view and in method of approach, there is no fundamental difference in intellectual character, certainly no inferiority. The ethnologist and the sociologist re-enforce the opinion of the empirical observer. Their judgment is that the distinction between the Oriental and the Occidental lies in technique and in knowledge, not in intellectual caliber. It is because the conception of life's values held by the Chinese is so different from that of Western peoples, that they have failed to develop modern technique and scientific knowledge. Now that they have come to place a new value upon these, there can be no doubt that rapid and fundamental changes will result.

Progress is largely the product of intelligence; while intelligence is the product of intellect and knowledge, just as physical force is the resultant of mass and momentum. The Chinese as a people possess the mass but not the momentum. If modern scientific knowledge be added to the intellectual qualities which the Chinese possess, the result will be one which the Western world cannot but respect and value.

The recent achievements of the Japanese in various lines of endeavor, militant, commercial, scientific, are excellent illustrations. It may be that these products of modern life are of no more intrinsic value to the Oriental peoples than those traits of character and products of social activity which they have held from time immemorial to be of fundamental value. But the Western world sets the higher value on these recent achievements, and the Orient is coming to the same opinion.

A nation that has preserved its identity by peaceful means for three milleniums; that has made the soil produce subsistence for a multitudinous population during that long period, while Western peoples have worn out their soil in less than as many centuries; that has produced many of the most influential of modern inventions, such as printing, gunpowder, and the compass; that has developed such mechanical ingenuity and commercial ability as are shown in its everyday life, undoubtedly possesses the ability to accomplish results by the use of methods worked out by the Western world. When modern scientific knowledge is added by the Chinese to the skill which they already have in agriculture, in commerce, in industry, in government, and in military affairs, results will be achieved on the basis of their physical stamina and moral qualities, which will remove the ignorance, the indifference, and the prejudice of the Western world regarding things Chinese.

This volume by Dr. Kuo will add to the understanding which his own people have of the task which is before them as well as to the knowledge which the Western world has of these changes now going on in the Orient—changes which are of concern and, let us hope, of profit to both.

TEACHERS COLLEGE,
COLUMBIA UNIVERSITY.

PAUL MONROE.

THE CHINESE SYSTEM

OF

PUBLIC EDUCATION

INTRODUCTION

The development of the educational system of China is a subject full of deep and varied interest to all students, whether of history, of politics, or of education. From it one might be able to trace the causes operating at an early period of the world's history to lead the people of China to so high a degree of civilization and to hold in unity as a nation so many millions of people. One might also be able to trace from it the method used to insure the perpetuity of the government and the content of the people. The way in which China's educational system has helped her to mold the character of the people, giving them a cohesion and a stability remarkable among the nations of the world, and the manner in which she is now struggling to adapt herself to modern conditions and to meet new demands, are also full of practical lessons for statesmanlike educators of all nations. Indeed, a record of even the mistakes and failures made by China would be some contribution to the educational world, for it might prevent other nations from falling into similar errors and warn them to guard against similar mistakes. In a word, the story of the development of education in China, like that of other nations, possesses points of interest and lessons in management valuable either positively as models for guidance or negatively as experiments to be avoided.

In the following pages no attempt, however, has been made to write a complete history of Chinese education, for to do so one would have to include in its vast development the record of the intellectual and moral culture of the Chinese people, or a resumé of their life in its diverse manifestations, literary and scientific, religious and political. He must, moreover, determine the causes, so numerous and so diverse, which have acted upon their character and shaped their educational institutions. What we have attempted to do is merely to make a critical survey of the development of the Chinese public educational system from the earliest time to the present period of rapid and startling transition. By the term "public educational system" is meant the system of schools maintained and controlled by the government for the education of the people. Strictly speaking, it does not include the civil service examination system, with which education in China is often identified, although the development of the one has been closely bound up with the development of the other. By the nature of the term, it does not even include the system of schools controlled by private individuals, which has played an important part in the development of Chinese education, for education in China has been, to a great extent, left to private initiative. Such being the limitation, the civil service examination system and the system of schools maintained by private individuals are therefore given a subordinate place in the course of this study. Indeed, they are mentioned only as they help to explain the evolution of the Chinese public educational system. Although the field of this investigation is so limited, the character of the study is nevertheless general rather than specific, extensive rather than intensive. This plan is adopted deliberately for the simple reason that at present the need for a work giving a comprehensive view of Chinese educational history is much greater than for one embodying the result of an intensive study of some single stage of the Chinese educational development.

Students of the history of education must have been struck by the fact that among the many influences which have shaped the destiny of education in Europe and America none have been so strong as those of religion and government. These two factors have also been the dominant influences in shaping the destiny of Chinese education. In the course of our inquiry we shall see that Confucianism, Buddhism, Taoism, and in recent years Christianity, have all directly or indirectly exerted their share of influence upon the educational system throughout its course of development. We shall also note that the political consideration has been strong from the very beginning of

China's history. Indeed, it may be said that the safety and perpetuity of the state have been the motives at the back of almost every educational effort put forth by the government. The fact is that the educational system is a political institution maintained by the state for the cultivation and promulgation of national ideals in order that safety and stability might be secured. Every school has been likened to a machine deliberately contrived by the state for the manufacture of the kind of citizens which it wishes to have. In democratic states future rulers must be trained; in military states future soldiers. Thus each country brings forth through its educational institutions a type of men and women characteristic of itself.

In addition to religion and government, we must mention at least one other dominant factor which has influenced the development of Chinese education, namely, the reverence for antiquity. This high respect for the past, characteristic of the Chinese people, fixed the gaze of ages upon past glory instead of upon future progress. Two causes may be assigned for this state of affairs. The first is unfamiliarity with the law of progress. For thousands of years the people labored in such a way as to give the impression that the older the civilization the better it is, and that everything will be achieved when the condition of antiquity is once restored. The second cause is undue respect for the ancient sages, who were held in such a high degree of veneration that people had the idea that they must imitate their example in everything they do or say, otherwise their sin would be indeed great. The three factors here suggested, viz., religion, government, and reverence for antiquity, have sometimes hastened the progress of education and sometimes impeded its progress. They have in one way or another shaped the destiny of Chinese education.

Chinese institutions are an expression of Chinese character and, in turn, Chinese character is reflected in Chinese institutions, especially those of education. Thus the people of China have been democratic in spirit; so has been their educational system. Under the traditional system, persons of almost every rank or class of society could become candidates for degrees. It often happened that the humblest subject in the land climbed, by sheer ability, to the highest round of the official ladder. This same democratic spirit is now being manifested in the modern educational system. The new schools provided by the government, as well as those provided by the people, are intended for all and are being utilized by all classes of society. At least there are as yet no sharp and well-defined schools intended for sharply defined classes of people, such as we find in Germany and, to some extent, in England and France. Indeed, in this respect China is rather more advanced than America, for even here the tendency of the upper classes of society to send their children to special schools, under one pretext or another, is still evident, especially in the East.

Again, the Chinese, like the English and the Germans, are known as highly conservative, and their educational system has also been conservative in character. The conservative element in the national character of the Chinese is well illustrated by the fact that the examination system, the Imperial Academy, and several other educational institutions had an almost unbroken existence for many centuries. The conservatism of the Chinese, however, has its limits. The important changes which the examination system and other educational institutions have undergone prove that they are by no means so fettered by tradition as to be incapable of welcoming improvements. They may be slow in making a new departure, but once the truth strikes home and its practicability is demonstrated, they do not hesitate at the radical nature of the change, nor are they discouraged by the difficulties and obstructions in the way. The two characteristics here suggested will be fully illustrated in the course of our present study.

In estimating the worth of the system of education of a foreign country, one naturally and unconsciously is led to compare it with the system of one's own country. Here we may raise the question: What is to be the standard of comparison? Whatever may be the answer, it seems certain that in making comparisons between two systems of education our judgment does not depend upon an a priori set of conditions, but upon the suitability of each to its environment. For the question is not which is the better system, but which system is better suited to its social and political background. It is only through keeping in mind the setting of a system that one is enabled to give a true estimate of its worth. Without weighing the environment one is apt to judge a system according to ideal standards which can be applied only to a system existing under ideal conditions. In judging China's modern educational system one has also to bear in mind that the policy of providing modern education upon a national basis was not adopted till a few years ago, and that she has not had as much time to develop it to a high degree of perfection as have the other nations. When due allowance is made for this it will be seen that China compares favorably with the best record found in the educational history of the world.

But when all allowances are made, there still remains doubt as to whether the systems of education are after all really comparable. Indeed, it has been declared by more than one writer on comparative education that the really vital elements of two systems of education cannot be directly compared. To quote Hughes, "We can place in juxtaposition tables and statistics showing the comparative costs of schoolhouses, payments of teachers and other officers, the relative amounts paid for educational purposes by each citizen, the amount spent on each child's training in the school, the regularity with which the children attend, the relative efficiency of the school laws, the relative facilities for higher training, and many other items; but the really vital question is not touched by such figures. For the question is, "Which of these systems of national training makes the best citizen?" and when the question is put thus one sees that its answer depends entirely upon what the phrase "best citizen" may connote. The phrase in France or Germany certainly does not imply the same attributes as in England or America, so that it is immediately evident how difficult, if not impossible, it is to answer such a question as "Which is the better educational system,—that of Germany or of England?"[1] Our consideration then leads to some such conclusion as this: that unless one takes extreme precautions, it is safer to let the system of China stand upon its own merits, remembering that any national system of training to be successful must meet national needs.

The question may be reasonably raised as to why China has been behind other nations in adopting a modern system of education providing training for all her citizens. The answer is, there was no necessity for it. For centuries China, secluded

[1] Hughes: The Making of Citizens, p. 4.

by sea, mountain, and desert, was prevented from coming into contact with western nations. With no railways or steamboats, telegraph or telephone, and few, if any, newspapers, life was simple and limited. Each community was a world by itself. The traditional system of education was sufficient to insure the safety of the nation and the content of the people. The introduction of mechanical inventions of steam power and railway which came with the advent of merchants and missionaries from western countries made the Chinese see the possibility of a fuller and richer life. Moreover, the forced contact with the outside nations, the humiliations which China suffered, and the birth of a new nationalism, made it necessary to change all her social, political, and educational institutions, in order to enable her to withstand troubles from within and foes from without.

It is perhaps not out of place to recall here that the movement for national training is a comparatively recent one even in western countries, and that it did not attain any considerable growth until the nineteenth century. It is true that national systems of education had existed in some countries long before the modern era, but they were not comprehensive and national in any such sense as they are to-day. However, the necessity for such a training had long before been recognized by great minds, such as Luther, Knox, Mulcaster, and a score of other great educators.

Finally it must be observed that while China has been slow in introducing reforms in her educational system she has always regarded education as of the highest importance. Writers on China's recent zeal for modern education have often spoken as though a great change had taken place in the attitude of the Chinese people toward education. This desire for western learning, however, does not represent quite such a change as at first appears. The spirit shown is really the same old spirit which has characterized China for many centuries, namely, high respect for learning. The change is not in the essence of the spirit, but in the character of the learning which that spirit admires. It used to admire the literary and ethical excellencies of the ancient Chinese classics; it now extends its admiration to the practical realities and usefulness of western science, because it recognizes therein the instruments for the realization of its new national and patriotic ideals.

CHAPTER I

ORIGIN OF THE ANCIENT EDUCATIONAL SYSTEM (2357–1122 B.C.)

Beginnings of Educational Effort

The beginnings of education in China can be traced as far back as the very beginning of her civilization, to a time when her social and political organizations were just emerging from the earliest stages of development. At that epoch, that which constituted the education of the people was general in character, simple in form, and devoid of the complex organization characteristic of education in more highly developed stages of culture and civilization. People were then either still passing through the period of hunting and nomadic life or in the first period of settled life, and the training they gave to the young was chiefly in the acquisition of various means for satisfying the bodily wants, such as hunting, fishing, the keeping of flocks, and the cultivation of the fields. The individual received such training through his daily experience, through the experience of his family, and that of his tribe or clan. The aim of education, conscious or otherwise, was to devise means for the profitable use of the environment and for increasing the productivity of the material resources.

The earliest authentic record of educational institutions of a consciously organized character dates as far back as the time of the two ancient rulers, Yao and Shun (2357–2205 B.C.), whose reigns not only mark an advanced stage in the development of the political, social, and intellectual life of the ancient Chinese, but are considered as one of the most brilliant and perfect epochs in Chinese history, resembling the period of the Antonines in the history of the Roman Empire. During these reigns and in the two dynasties which immediately follow, namely those of Hsia (2205–1766 B.C.) and Shang (1766–1122 B.C.), we see not only the origin of the civil service examination system, which plays an important part in the history of Chinese education, but also the origin of state educational offices and the beginnings of schools and colleges which soon developed into a com plete system of schools the like of which one can scarcely find in the long history of Chinese education until we come to our own day.

Institution of the Examination System

The ancient educational system of China is closely bound up with the competitive examination system whose object was to provide men of ability for the service of the state. The latter system, however, originally started with testing the ability of those already in office and runs back in its essential features to the earliest period of recorded history.[1] The germ from which it sprang was a maxim of the ancient sages which is expressed in the following words, "Employ the able and promote the worthy," and examinations were resorted to as affording the best test of ability and worth. Of the Great Shun, that model emperor of remote antiquity, it is recorded that he examined his officers every third year, and after three examinations either gave them promotion or dismissed them from service.[2] On what subjects he examined them at a time when letters were but newly invented and when books were as yet rare,[3] we are not told, neither are we told whether he subjected candidates to any test previous to appointment; yet the mere holding of such a periodical examination established a precedent which continued to be observed even to modern times.

Creation of Offices of Public Education

To the ancient sovereign Shun, the "Book of History" has also given the credit of having created among the nine administrative offices of the realm at least three offices of an educational character.[4] He appointed Hsieh as minister of education (Ssŭtu), to teach the people the duties of the five human rela-

---

[1] The examinations are of two kinds, which have been distinguished as pre-official and post-official; the former is the offspring of the latter, which it has outgrown and overshadowed.

[2] Legge: The Chinese Classics, Vol. III, Part I, p. 50.

[3] The books of this early period are made of tablets of bamboo upon which characters are traced with a stylus. Some Chinese historians are wont to claim that a large number of books recording the events of and belonging to dynasties preceding the period of Yao and Shun were in existence, but such claims are unsupported by any trustworthy evidences.

[4] Legge: The Chinese Classics, Vol. III, Part I, pp. 47–48.

tionships, namely, the relationships between sovereign and subject, parent and child, husband and wife, elder and younger brother, and between friends. He also appointed Baron I as minister of religion to direct the three religious ceremonies[5] and Kwei as director of music. These state offices of education having their origin in the time of Yao and Shun were also found during the time of the first two dynasties, Hsia and Shang, not only in the capital of the kingdom but also in the capitals of the various feudal states, at least in the larger ones.[6] This record of public educational offices existing alongside of other ministries of the state is significant in that it reveals the fact that from the earliest time education or the provision for education was recognized in China as a function of the government. This explains in part why China had some sort of consciously organized system of education long before any other Asiatic or European people.

Earliest Schools and Colleges on Record

During the reigns of Yao and Shun there were in existence near the Imperial Palace at least two kinds of educational institutions, one called Shang Hsiang, and the other Hsia Hsiang. The former was a college devoted to higher education or Ta Hsüeh, and the latter was a college for lower education or Siao Hsüeh. These institutions also existed during the dynasties of Hsia and Shang, but were then known by different names. During the Hsia dynasty they were known respectively as Tung Hsü, or College of the East, and Hsi Hsü, or College of the West. The College of the East was situated, as the name indicates, at the east of the Imperial Palace, and the College of the West was in the western precincts of the capital. During the Shang dynasty they were respectively known as Yu Hsüeh, or College of the Right, and Tso Hsüeh, or College of the Left, the former situated in the western precincts of the capital, and the latter to the east of the Imperial Palace, holding positions the reverse of those held by the same institutions during the preceding dynasty. These two kinds of institutions

---

5 The three religious ceremonies are all the observances in the worship of the spirit of Heaven, the spirit of the earth, and the spirits of the dead. Legge: The Chinese Classics, Vol. III, Part I, p. 47.

6 Legge: The Chinese Classics, Vol. IV, Part II, p. 301.

were devoted to the education of the princes and the sons of nobles and officials, as well as the promising youths of the common people. A custom was in vogue during those early dynasties of supporting or entertaining with feasts the aged of the *state* in the college for higher education and the aged of the *people* in the college for lower education.[7] The sovereign made regular visits to these institutions to pay his respects to the aged men gathered there, and to discuss with them the problems of the state. Certain ceremonies were performed during those visits and these gave rise to a system of dances and music.

One finds, also, a record of the existence of other kinds of educational institutions during that early antiquity, such as Hsiao, Hsü, Hsiang Hsüeh, and Ku Tsung. Hsiao, meaning teaching, is a name given to the schools existing during the Hsia dynasty for the education of the children of the common people. Hsü, meaning archery, is the name used to designate the same kind of schools existing during the Shang dynasty. Hsiang Hsüeh is the name given to a kind of educational institution that was in existence in the departments (hsiang) of the feudal states. The last mentioned institution, Ku Tsung, had its origin also in the Shang dynasty. The word Ku, originally meaning blind, is generally understood to mean musician, and the word Tsung signifies honor. Ku Tsung then means the hall where one renders honor to the blind, that is, the musicians. This institution was situated near the Imperial Palace and in it music and ceremonies were at first taught.

Content of Ancient Education

The character of the ancient educational offices and of the earliest schools and colleges reveals the fact that the content of education in early antiquity consisted chiefly of rituals (li), music, and lessons on the duties of the five human relationships or the Five Humanities (Wu-lun). Rituals originally included only the observances in the worship of the spirit of Heaven, the spirit of the earth, and the spirits of the dead. They enabled the individual to become familiar with forms of worship, which

---

[7] The aged of the *state* (or Kuo-lau) included officials and others distinguished by their virtues, while the aged of the *people* (or Shu-lau) included fathers and grandfathers of those who died in public service, as well as those whose only claim was age.

played an important part in the public and private life of the ancient people, since they believed that their happiness and prosperity depended greatly upon the sustaining of a right relationship with the spirits of the dead and that this right relationship was dependent upon proper forms of worship. In course of time, however, the term li came to include all religious and social usages, manners, customs, as well as laws of the land, such as we find embodied in the Book of Rites (Li-chi), Ceremonial Rites of Chou (Chou-li), and Decorum Ritual (I-li). The word ceremony, often regarded as the equivalent of the word li, does not at all convey the true import of the word, for li includes not only the external conduct, but also involves the right principles from which all true etiquette and politeness spring. The policy of the government, the organization of the family, and the rules of society, are all founded on the true li. In explanation of the importance of the three works on the subject of li or ritual, M. Callery shows in a few words what a wide field is covered: "Li epitomizes the entire Chinese mind, and, in my opinion, the Li-chi is *per se* the most exact and complete monograph that China has been able to give of itself to other nations. Its affections, if it has any, are satisfied by li; its duties are fulfilled by li; its virtues and vices are referred to li; the natural relations of created beings essentially link themselves in li—in a word, to that people li is man as a moral, political, and religious being in his multiplied relations with family, country, society, morality, and religion."[8]

Next to li or rituals comes music, which includes poetry and songs as well as dancing and instrumental music. The book of odes (Shi-ching), which is a collection of rhymed ballads in various metres, composed between the reign of the Great Yü, the founder of the Hsia dynasty, and the beginning of the sixth century B.C., throws much light upon the character of music in the period under consideration. A number of musical instruments are mentioned in the odes. Among them are the flute, the drum, the bell, the lute, and the Pandean pipes. The ballads or odes are arranged under the following heads: (a) ballads commonly sung by the people in the various feudal states and forwarded periodically by the nobles to their suzerain,

---

[8] Legge: The Chinese Classics, Vol. III, Part I, p. 47.

the Son of Heaven[9]; (b) odes sung at ordinary entertainment given by the suzerain; (c) odes sung on grand occasions when the feudal nobles were gathered together; (d) panegyrics and sacrificial odes. Many of the ballads and odes deal with warfare, and with the separation of wives from husbands; others with agriculture and the chase, with marriage and feasting. To these may be added those containing complaints against the harshness of officials, as well as against the ordinary sorrows of life. Of dancing, the Book of Rites mentions at least four kinds which had to be performed in the great ceremonies. They are called dances with the shield, with the lance, with the plume, and with the flute, each named after the nature of the object which the dancer holds in his hand.[10]

The function of music was to mold the temper and the character of the individual, enabling him to be in harmony with his fellow-beings and with the spirits.[11] Thus in the appointment of Kwei as director of music, Shun is recorded to have enjoined him to teach music to the youth of the land, so that "the straightforward may yet be mild, the gentle may yet be dignified, the strong not tyrannical, and the impetuous not arrogant." To the same ruler is credited the following conception of the function of music: "Poetry is the expression of earnest thought; singing is the prolonged utterance of that expression. The notes accompany that utterance, and they are harmonized by the pitch pipes. In this way the eight different kinds of instruments can all be adjusted so that one shall not take from or interfere with another, and spirits and men will thereby be brought into harmony."[12]

The Five Humanities as already observed deal with the duties belonging to the relationships between parent and child, sovereign and subject, husband and wife, elder brother and younger brother, friend and friend. These relationships, according

---

[9] The ballads so forwarded were then submitted to the imperial musicians, who were able to judge from the nature of such compositions what would be the manners and customs prevailing in the state, and to advise the suzerain accordingly as to the good or bad administration of each vassal ruler.

[10] Li Chi Chu Shu, Vol. XX, p. 5.

[11] Gützlaff, in his history of China, speaking of music as a means of inspiring the softer feelings of nature, and of promoting harmony amongst the nations, suggests that the music of the ancient Chinese must have been far superior to that of their posterity, for the Chinese music of modern times is not productive of the effect which it seems once to having exercised.

[12] Legge: The Chinese Classics, Vol. III, Part I, p. 48.

to Mencius, should be guided respectively by the principles of love, righteousness, propriety, deference, and sincerity.[13] The belief was that with these principles inculcated in the minds of the people they would live at peace with one another and social stability would thus be secured.

It seems clear that the content of education during the time of Yao and Shun and the first two dynasties, Hsia and Shang, was essentially moral and religious in character, dealing as it does with the relationship between man and man and between man and spirits. The existence of the institution known as Hsü, where archery was practiced and taught, seems to indicate that some form of physical or military training was also given. Literary education, as we understand it to-day, hardly existed at that early epoch, when the art of printing was not yet discovered. It is recorded, however, that in the Shang Hsiang, or college for higher education, the study of bamboo books and the tracing of characters on bamboo tablets were among the occupations of its students.[14]

Method of Ancient Education

The method of education of the ancient Chinese, like that used by the ancients of other nations, was simple in character. As yet there was no large body of knowledge or organized subjects of study through which the aims of education could be realized. Although bamboo books are recorded to have existed at that time, their use was confined, as we have seen, to the Shang Hsiang, or college of higher education, and their number must have been very small, owing to the difficulties involved in their preparation. The moral training and the training in ceremonials and music were given chiefly in two ways, by word of mouth and by example. In the description of the training of a boy given in the Regulations of the Interior, in the Book of Rites, we read that in the performance of ceremonials and usages of the school the master commences and the children follow his movements. Again, history conveys to us the idea that the ancient rulers and teachers ruled and influenced the people not so much by their teachings as by their personal character and conduct. It appears from these instances that

---

[13] Mencius, Book IV, Pt. I, Chap. 4, Sec. 8.
[14] Li Chi Chu Shu, Vol. XX, p. 5.

the method of teaching by example received great emphasis and that imitation, which is one of the effective methods of acquisition, played an important part in the education of the ancient people. Experience and observation somehow taught those ancient Chinese the psychological principle that man naturally and unconsciously molds his life according to the models he admires, and hence that personal example, especially in regard to morals and manners, is often superior to advice and orders, because the model given often tells the individual more clearly what to do, or makes him more inclined to do it, than mere words could possibly do.

Aims of Ancient Education

We have observed that at the dawn of civilization the aim of education, whether conscious or otherwise, was merely to devise means for the profitable use of environment and for increasing the productivity of material resources. By the time of Yao and Shun and the dynasties of Hsia and Shang, however, society had reached a high degree of development which caused a change in the motives of educational efforts. The aim of education, now clearly conceived and definitely formulated, was to enable the individual to live peaceably with his fellow-beings and to maintain the stability of the state. This twofold aim of education is embodied in the familiar Chinese expression "Hsiu Chi Chih Jen," meaning to cultivate one's self and to govern others. To cultivate one s self involves the application of the principles of the five human relationships in one's daily life, and to govern others consists in making rituals and music effective in the control of public and private life.[15] Stated in more general terms the aim of education was to develop the individual into a man of virtue and culture, and to secure social control through raising up leaders with ability and character to influence the lives of others. These aims have continued to be the motives of Chinese education throughout China's history of many centuries.

---

[15] Chiao Yu Shih, p. 1; Chih Na Chiao Yu Shih, p. 2.

CHAPTER II

ANCIENT EDUCATIONAL SYSTEM AND ITS DECADENCE

DYNASTIES OF CHOU (1122–255 B.C.) AND CHIN (255–206 B.C.)

Under the benign influence of the founders of the Chou dynasty, Wen Wang, Wu Wang, and Chou Kung, whose erudition, integrity, patriotism, and inventions place them among the most distinguished men of antiquity, Chinese institutions, both social and political, made rapid advance, and by the time the Chou dynasty was at its period of greatest prosperity, China had already reached the zenith of her civilization. Great progress had been made in government, science, education, and philosophy, and an era of great refinement and culture, bearing resemblance to the Periclean age of the Grecian history, had been ushered in. In the meantime, the ancient educational system, the beginnings of which we have already traced, had developed along with other institutions to such a stage of perfection that it actually provided popular as well as higher education. This system, being regarded as the best educational system China ever had, has always been referred to with passionate admiration by the Chinese people of after generations. Such being the case, the system deserves to be considered somewhat in detail. We shall first examine the system at its best and then notice the change during its stages of decadence and transition.

Name, Location, and Character of Schools

Speaking generally, there were in existence during the time of the Chou dynasty two sets of schools, one of which was found in the capital of the king and in the capital cities of the feudal states, and the other in the feudal states at large. Those which come under the former category were five in number, namely, Shang Hsiang, Tung Hsü, Ku Tsung, Cheng Chun, and Pi Yung. Shang Hsiang derived its name from the college for higher education, established during the reign of Shun. During the Chou dynasty this institution was situated in the western suburb of the Palace in the northern part of the capital. It was a school devoted to lower education, which included reading and writing. This institution is sometimes called Mi-lin or granary of rice, because it was used to store the supplies of grain dedicated to sacrifice. In this institution the aged of the *people* were entertained by the sovereign. Tung Hsü, or College of the East, derived its name from the college for higher education, of the Hsia dynasty, and was sometimes called Tung Chiao. It was situated in the eastern suburb of the capital to the right of the Palace, and was an institution devoted to higher education, or Ta Hsüeh, where rituals and various kinds of dances were taught. In this college the aged of the *state* were entertained by the sovereign. We recognize Ku Tsung as having originated in the dynasty of Shang, it being a musical gymnasium where the students were taught to sing songs, to play musical instruments, and to perform the various rituals. Cheng Chun, or College of Perfection and Equalization, had its origin in the Chou dynasty, and was devoted to higher education. It received its name because it perfected that which was lacking in the students, and equalized that which was excessive or defective in them. This college was situated in the southern part of the capital. The last named institution, Pi Yung, was situated in the center of the capital. Regarding the exact nature of this institution there is much uncertainty. Some regard it as merely a field of military exercise, like the field of Mars of ancient Rome; others think it was a kind of quasi-educational institution where the sovereign met the ministers of state for conference concerning the affairs of the state.[1] According to Li-chou, a work published in 1092 under the Sung dynasty and cited by Ma-tuan-lin, Pi Yung was identified with the College of Perfection and Equalization which we have mentioned as an institution devoted to higher education. In the section Wen Wang Shih Chih of the Book of Rites, the name Cheng Chun first appears to designate a school of higher learning; later the name Pi Yung was employed for a similar purpose,

[1] The two words Pi and Yung are represented by two different sets of characters in the Book of Poetry and the Book of Rites, and can thus admit different interpretations.

and the name Cheng Chun ceased to be used. It is quite possible then that the two names representing the same institution for higher learning existed during different times of the same dynasty. However, most writers seem to favor the interpretation making Cheng Chun and Pi Yung two distinct institutions. Thus the imperial edition of the Book of Rites gives a chart illustrating the position of each of the five institutions. Pi Yung is represented as being in the center of the capital; Cheng Chun in the south; Shang Hsiang in the north; Tung Hsü in the east; and Ku Tsung in the west. The name Pi Yung was reserved to designate the college in the imperial capital, and the corresponding institution found in the capital cities of feudal states was known as Pan Kung.

Regarding schools existing in the feudal states during the Chou dynasty, we are told that each hamlet (lü) had halls of study called Shu; each village (tang) had a school called Hsiang or Hsü; each district (chou) had a school called Hsü; each department of a state (hsiang) had a college called Hsiang.[2] Shu re ers to the two halls of study which were found on the sides of a gate situated at the entrance of the street composing the little village lü. According to the usage of the people of the time of Chou, each day, after the opening of the work of the spring, all the inhabitants of each village, men and women, in going out to the fields in the morning and in returning home in the evening, received instruction in the halls of study. The instruction was given by men of strong moral character chosen from the former officers of the state, who retired from public service upon reaching the age of seventy. The village school is sometimes called Hsiang, and sometimes called Hsü. Both of these names were carried over from the schools of former dynasties. The district school called Hsü also derived its name from the dynasty of Hsia when it represented a kind of gymnasium for instruction and practice of archery. The name Hsiang, given to the college of each department of each feudal state, had its origin in the time of Shun, when it was a college of higher education.

---

[2] According to the system adopted by the Chou dynasty for the division of the people, every twenty-five families make one lü; every 500 families make one tang; five tang, or 2,500 families, make one chou; five chou, or 120,000 families, make one hsiang; and a number of hsiang make up one principality or feudal state. The number of hsiang which make up each principality changes from time to time.

Content of Education

In the description of the various schools of the imperial capital and those of the capital cities of the feudal states, we have observed that reading and writing were taught in Shang Hsiang, dancing was taught in Tung Hsü, rituals were taught in Ku Tsung, and music in Cheng Chun. These represent merely special subjects taught to princes and to sons of nobles and officers. In addition, students were given training in ethical ideas and in personal morality, as well as poetry, mathematics, archery, charioteering, and various other arts useful in the life of the time. The whole curriculum of the time of the Chou dynasty, according to the section on Department of Earth (Ti-kuan) of the Book of Rites, is expressed in the following terms: the six virtues, the six praiseworthy actions, and the six arts. The six virtues are wisdom, benevolence, goodness, righteousness, loyalty, and harmony. The six praiseworthy actions are honoring one's parents, being friendly to one's brothers, being neighborly, maintaining cordial relationships with relatives through marriages, being trustful, and being sympathetic. The six arts, which correspond to the Trivium and Quadrivium of the medieval schools, consist of rituals, music, archery, charioteering, writing, and mathematics. A liberal education includes five kinds of ritual, five kinds of music, five ways of archery, five ways of directing a chariot, six kinds of writings, and nine operations of mathematics. Judged from the modern point of view the training was moral, physical, and intellectual in character, and closely related to life, preparing, as it did, the individual to participate in the daily activities of life. The ideal of education of the time of Chou seems to have been the harmonious and symmetrical development of the body and mind, and may be said to represent a combination of Spartan and Athenian ideals of education, which called for a training at once intellectual and moral, as well as physical and military.

The chapter entitled Regulations of the Interior (Nei-tse) of the Book of Rites contains a description of the life of a boy and a girl in ancient times, which not only gives a more vivid picture of the exact nature of education, but also shows the difference between the training of a boy and that of a girl. This description when translated reads as follows:

Career of a Boy

At six years of age the child is taught the numbers (1, 10, 100, 1000, 10,000) and the names of the points of the compass. At seven years of age the boys and the girls do not sit on the same mat; they do not eat together. At eight years of age, children should follow the older persons in entering and going out of the gate of the house, in sitting upon the mat, and in drinking and eating. They begin to be taught to show deference, that is, to give precedence to others.

At nine years the youth is taught to distinguish days (the first day of the month, the day of the full moon, and the names of the days in the cycle of sixty). At ten years the youths go out, and commence to engage in occupations outside the house. They dwell for a certain time away from home to study writing and mathematics. For their clothing, they do not wear pure silk. In the performance of ceremonial rites and in the usages of the school the master commences and the children follow his movements. In the morning and in the evening they study the practices and habits of children of ten years. They ask questions of those who are older; they trace characters upon tablets of bamboo and learn to pronounce them.

At thirteen years of age they study music; they read aloud songs in verse. They dance the dance "Cho." When they have completed fifteen years, they dance the dance "Siang." They learn archery and charioteering.

At twenty years the young man becomes of age. He commences to study the rituals. He can wear clothing made of fur and of pure silk; he executes the dance of Ta-hia (instituted by Yu). He practices sincerely filial piety and fraternal love; he extends his acquaintances, but he teaches not (because he fears that his ideas may not yet be sufficiently pure). He keeps to himself, and does not push himself forward.

At thirty years he marries; he commences to perform the duties of the man (i.e., he receives a field to cultivate, and fulfills the duties toward the state). He extends his studies, but not regularly (if he has a subject which pleases him, then he studies). He enters into league with his friends and compares the purity of their intentions.

At forty years of age he commences to enter into public offices of the second order; according to the nature of affairs, he expresses his opinions, he produces his observations; if the orders of superiors are conformable to good rules, then he fulfills his duty and obeys; if they are not, then he withdraws himself from public service.

At fifty years of age he receives the higher insignia, becomes a prefect, and enters into the offices of the first order. At sixty years of age he withdraws from public affairs.

Career of a Girl

The girl, at the age of ten, no longer goes out of the house;[3] as soon as she reaches this age, she remains at home. The instructress teaches her to be polite and modest, to listen and obey. The girl occupies herself with roping the hemp and silk and in weaving. She learns to do the work of women, such as the making of clothing. She supervises the family sacrifices; she brings the wine, the extracted juices, the baskets and earthen vessels, the macerated plants, and the minced meats. In the performance of rites, she helps to place the objects to be offered.

At fifteen years of age she pins up her hair (if she is betrothed) at twenty years she marries. If she loses her father or mother at this age, she marries at twenty-three years of age. If it is a regular marriage she becomes a legitimate wife; if it is a marriage without formalities, she becomes a concubine.

The descriptions just given indicate plainly the separation of the studies of boys and girls after the age of ten. The girls were then obliged to remain inside the house, occupying themselves only with the duties usually assigned to women;[4] and judging from the silence of the Book of Rites, they learned neither reading and writing nor mathematics. In fact, this kind of knowledge is mentioned only in the studies of male children, and is given to them only after they have reached the age of ten years. These facts are sufficient to show that during the Chou dynasty there was little opportunity provided for the intellectual training of women. This is not to be taken, however, to mean that the people of ancient China did not realize the importance of

---

[3] This usage no doubt refers to girls of the upper class, for in connection with the village schools we have observed that it was customary in the time of Chou for men and women to go out into the fields to work after the opening of the spring season.

[4] This statement is borne out by other documentary evidences. For example, one reads in the Book of Odes that a girl learns how to prepare the wine and how to cook food, and that she endeavors not to be burdensome to her parents.

women's education, but rather to indicate that intellectual training was not regarded as an essential part of women's education because their sphere of duty is limited to the home. In the education of women great emphasis was laid on the up-building of moral conduct and on the inculcation of feminine virtues. It is recorded in the Ceremonial Rites of Chou that the imperial wives systematized the laws for educating females in order that the ladies of the Palace might be instructed in morals, conversation, manners, and work, and that in the good old times of Chou, the virtuous women set such an excellent example that it influenced the customs not only of that time, but also of later generations.[5] This moral ideal of education for women has persisted throughout the long centuries of China's history and has been influential in molding the lives of her women and in elevating them to the high position which they hold in the family and in society.

Method of Education

In accordance with the chapters Hsüeh Chi and Nei-tse of the Book of Rites, which contain numerous passages touching upon education, the principles of instruction held by the ancient Chinese are extremely modern in character, revealing a keen insight into the true nature of the human mind. Mere memory work, characteristic of Chinese education in later generations, was strongly condemned. Education was not regarded as an artificial procedure by which one comes into possession of formal knowledge of some sort, but as the process of development of the individual from within. We are told that learning should proceed from the easy to the difficult, from the coarse to the fine; that transition from one step to another should be gradual rather than sudden; and that great things should be accomplished through the accumulation of many small things. Again, one should concentrate his attention upon one thing at a time, and should not scatter his thoughts. In the effort to learn, the student should be left to exert his own powers, so that his brain will not be injured and his spirit of independence may not fail to be fully developed.

In addition to the information found in the Book of Rites, many of the aphorisms of Confucius also reveal something of

---

[5] Cf. Burton: The Education of Women, pp. 11-33.

the educational method of his time. On the importance of reasoning in the learning process, Confucius says, "Learning without thought is labor lost, and if one learns only by memory and does not think, all remains dark." On self-activity, he says, "I shall not teach until the scholars desire to know something, and I do not help until the scholars need my help; if of the four corners of a thing I have shown and explained one corner and the scholars do not find for themselves the other three, I do not explain further." Confucius also seems to believe in the principle of leading upward from easy things to the difficult ones. Thus Yen Yu, speaking of the way in which he is taught by Confucius, says, "The kind master leads me step by step."

The sayings of Mencius also contain much that is suggestive of the early methods of education[6]. "The moral man," he says, "teaches in five ways. 1, There are some he influences, like a timely rain; 2, with some he perfects their virtue; 3, with some he brings out their talents; 4, of some he answers the questions; 5, some he teaches privately. These are the five methods which the moral man uses in teaching." In other words, every teacher should teach his pupils in various ways, according to their individuality. Of these five classes of students, the first, thoroughly awake to instruction, receive it eagerly and joyously; the second have more aptitude for the ethical and yield themselves to right guidance; the third have a special inclination for this or that theoretical or practical department and press on in that direction; the fourth are intellectual, critical natures whose questions should be answered lest, through suppressed doubts, they should end in uncertainty; the fifth are those who specially attach themselves to the master and allow themselves to be urged on by him.

Admission, Examination, Promotion

According to the Book of Rites the colleges in the Imperial Palace and in the capitals of feudal states were open not only to the hereditary princes and other sons of the sovereign and the eldest sons of different princes of the court, but also to the eldest sons of the ministers, eldest sons of officers called Ta-fu and Yuen-shih, as well as to the sons of the common people chosen from the kingdom at large upon the basis of their merit irrespective of their birth. Admission to the colleges was based upon merit

6 Giles, H. A.: The Work of Mencius.

determined through examination. The qualifications looked for in such examinations were virtue, ability in managing public affairs, and ease of expression. Students of the college for lower education who distinguished themselves were admitted to the College of Perfection and Equalization where they received one glass of wine from the hands of the sovereign as a token of distinction. On the other hand, those who failed to meet the requirements of the examination must continue to study for further examinations. It sometimes happened, however, that candidates who distinguished themselves in one of the required qualifications were also given admission to the college for higher learning.

According to the chapter Hsüeh Chi of the Book of Rites the students were examined every second year. In the first year an examination was given to test the ability of the student in analyzing ancient classics and in choosing the aim of life. In the third year an examination was given to test his perseverance in the pursuance of studies and his sociability among friends. In the fifth year the examination tested the extent of his learning and the intimacy of his acquaintance with his teacher. In the seventh year he was tested as to his way of treating knowledge and of choosing friends. By the time a student had satisfactorily met all the above requirements he was said to have reached "small perfection" (Siao Ch'êng). In the ninth year an examination was again given to see whether the student was able to classify things under their proper categories, whether he understood things thoroughly, was able to be independent, and was strong enough to withstand all evil influences. If he fulfilled the requirements of this last examination he was said to have reached "great perfection" (Ta Ch'êng).

A system of promotion from one grade of educational institution to another seems to have been in operation during the Chou dynasty. We are told that the students who distinguish themselves in the village schools are sent to the schools in the district; and those who distinguish themselves in the district schools are sent to the colleges in the department; finally, those who distinguish themselves in the departmental colleges are sent to the colleges in the capital city of the feudal prince, and the best of them to the colleges of the imperial capital. Fitting rank is given to the students as they advance from one institution to another as a badge of honor and distinction. The most worthy of the students in the colleges are given official rank and are chosen to fill administrative posts either in the departments and districts or in the capitals of the feudal states or the kingdom.

School Age, Term, and Year

There is a certain degree of uncertainty as to the age at which students were admitted into schools and colleges. Thus, according to Peh-huo-t'ung, a work of the first century of the Christian era, and several other works of equal importance, the hereditary prince enters the Siao Hsüeh or college for lower education at eight years of age, and the Ta Hsüeh or college for higher education at fifteen. According to Shang-shu-ta-chuen of Ma Yung, a work of the same epoch, the eldest sons of the imperial councillors and ministers as well as the eldest sons of certain classes of officers enter the Siao Hsüeh at the age of eighteen, and the Ta Hsüeh at the age of twenty. Biot concludes that the age of admission varies according to the social rank of the parents and that the reason why the sons of sovereigns and princes were admitted at an earlier age than the sons of officers is because the former surpassed the latter in intelligence. Most Chinese writers, however, believe that the age given in Peh-huo-t'ung is the correct one, that is, children enter the institution for lower education at eight and the institution for higher education at fifteen.

The exact length of each school term and year is not known, but there is much evidence to show that the four seasons were taken as units of the school year, and that due care was taken to see that the studies and occupations were adapted to the particular seasons in which they were placed. We learn, for example, that in spring and summer students practiced archery and various kinds of dances in Tung Hsü and recited songs in Ku Tsung; in autumn they gathered in Ku Tsung to learn rituals; in winter they learned to read and write in Shang Hsiang. A passage depicting the educational usage of the time of Chou, found in Shang-shu-ta-chuen of Ma Yung, furnishes further information concerning the point in question. The passage reads "When the plow has been placed under shelter, when the harvest has been taken in and the work of the year finished, all the young men not yet married enter school. At the winter solstice, they withdraw from the school for forty-five days to prepare for the work of agriculture."

School Offices

In the description of public officers of the Chou dynasty found in the Ceremonial Rites of Chou,[7] one finds mention of special officers charged with the duty of conducting the educational institutions at public expense and of teaching therein. Thus we are told that the teaching of rituals and dances was under the supervision of the directors of music; that reading and writing were given under the supervision of the director of study; that rituals were taught under the direction of the director of rituals and his assistants. According to the same authority, the director of music had also the duty of overseeing the studies in the kingdom, of gathering together students in schools, and of taking charge of the College of Perfection and Equalization. He and his assistant taught not only musical harmony, but also virtue, reading, and dancing. Other educational officers are also mentioned, including the Grand Instructor (Shih-chih) who taught the children of the state virtues and good conduct and the Conservator (Pao-chih) who taught the six arts. Both the Ceremonial Rites of Chou and the Book of Rites mention another officer attached to the ministry of war, known as Chou-tzŭ, whose duty was to gather together students in the proper schools according to the seasons of the year, to regulate their places in the dances which they perform, to direct them in their studies, and also to teach them paternal affection and brotherly love. This officer was thus a kind of preceptor charged with the task of guiding the pupils in their studies, and of exercising a direct inspection over them. Special officers engaged in teaching or conducting schools and colleges in the departments, districts, and villages are also mentioned, including departmental teacher (Hsiang-shih), father teacher (Fu-shih), and junior teacher (Shao-shih). Most of these were chosen among the virtuous old men who had retired from public service.

Number of Schools

Statistics concerning schools of that remote antiquity are naturally incomplete, but there are sufficient data to indicate

[7] Ceremonial Rites of Chou: Chapter Chou-kuan.

something of their extent in this golden age of Chinese educational history. According to Chou-li a certain feudal state alone had the following schools and colleges: six departmental colleges, thirty district schools, one hundred and fifty village schools, and three thousand schools found in small villages and hamlets.[8] When one multiplies these figures by the number of feudal states, one can get a rough estimate of the number of schools and colleges that were once in existence, provided that one takes into account the size of the various classes of feudal states. Exact statistics regarding feudal states are, however, not available. In T'ung Chien Kang Mu, the revised version of the famous historical work by Ssŭ Ma Kuang, known as T'ung Chien or Mirror of History, it is estimated that the number of feudal states after the ascension of Wu Wang, the first sovereign of the Chou dynasty, was seventy, and that the number continued to grow till it reached the eighteen hundred which are found in the official petitions made at the time of Han dynasty. This second figure, which reduces feudal states to the dimensions of mere districts, refers probably to the latter part of the Chou dynasty, when the great feudal states had been divided, as generations passed, into small states.

Administration of Education

The administration of education during the time of Chou was in the hands of the regular administrative officers of the government. The state of Chou, which was the representative state of the dynasty, had six departments for administrative purposes, namely, Celestial Department, Terrestrial Department, Department of Spring, Department of Summer, Department of Autumn, and Department of Winter.[9] The minister at the head of the Terrestrial Department, called Ta-ssŭ-tu, had charge of the supervision of public instruction in addition to other duties attached to the office, such as commerce, agriculture, and police. The minister of the Terrestrial Department accomplished his task through the various administrative heads of all the territorial divisions, who were required not only to administer laws but also to have general direction of

[8] Cf. Ho, Y. S.: Chinese Education, p. 18; Book of Rites, Chapter Wang Chih.

[9] The head of the Celestial Department, known as the Prime Minister (Ta-tsung-tsai), exercised a general control over the other five departments.

public instruction in their respective jurisdictions. It was customary for the head of the village and that of the district to gather the people together on certain days of the year to read the laws for their instruction. These officers also examined the moral conduct of the people, and their ability in the arts of war, for the purpose of encouragement and for the selection of men of ability to be sent to college for a higher education.

The Examination or Selective System (Hsüan Chü)

By the time of the Chou dynasty the system of selecting able men for public service had developed, along with the school system, to a higher degree of organization, including the examination of candidates as well as those already in office. Every three years an examination was held in each department, under the direction of officers and men who had reached old age, for the purpose of selecting capable and virtuous men to be prepared to assume the responsibilities of the government. The administrative head of each department, called Hsiang-ta-fu, recommended the successful candidates to the Ta-ssŭ-tu, the minister of the Terrestrial Department, who, after examining them, sent them to the college of the department or that of the capital. Those who distinguished themselves in the college of the department were called Siu-shih, meaning flourishing scholars who became officers in the department and district. They were under the control of the head of the department, and their ranking in the official ladder was determined by the Ta-ssŭ-tu. Those who distinguished themselves in the college of the capital were called Chin Shih, meaning promoted scholar, and were admitted to the higher offices of the kingdom, such as hou, ching, ta-fu, and ssu. Candidates for higher offices came under the control of the Great Director of Music, and their ranking in the official ladder was determined by the Minister of War (Ta-ssŭ-ma) through the insufficient test of archery. All the appointments were confirmed by the sovereign, who received periodical reports of the selection of men of merit and of all official appointments.

Those who were already in office were also tested periodically. The higher officers were required to record the deeds of their subordinates, to retain in office only those who were worthy, and to report to the prince the names of those so retained. The latter, after summoning these officers and examining them himself, put them to a test of public opinion. When a man had passed all the tests satisfactorily, he was promoted to a higher rank in his official career. There were then three stages of selection, first, selection by the heads of departments and districts; second, selection by higher officers; third, selection by the prince himself. Every third year the prince of each feudal state also presented a few selected men to the sovereign to fill positions in the imperial court. The number of men sent was determined by the rank of the state. The kingdom of the first class were entitled to present three candidates, the kingdoms of the second class two, and the kingdoms of the third class one candidate.

This system of selecting able men for office reveals at least four points of great significance. First, it shows that the system was democratic in spirit in that it was open to all those who possessed the necessary qualifications, irrespective of their birth, their position in society, or the amount of wealth they possessed. Next, it shows that the educational system, like the system of government, had a high degree of centralization. to which policy the Chou dynasty committed itself. Further more, it indicates clearly that the tests to which the candidate for office was put were based on real ability and moral characte and not on mere literary skill, as in the system of later generations. Finally, the record reveals the fact that during the period under consideration all officers were chosen from the colleges, and that the school system was not merely a stepping stone to the examination system as was the case in later generations. This last fact explains in part the reason why the school system during the Chou dynasty flourished and developed to such a high state of completeness that it occupied a position of great importance in the life of the nation.

Ancient School System in its Stages of Decadence and Transition

Beginning with the eighth century before the Christian era, there came a long period of decadence during which the base of the feudal system of Chou with their institutions became obliterated in the midst of general insubordination of the feudal princes. The imperial supremacy was no longer respected higher and lower education were totally neglected, and the princes, divided by continual wars, no longer occupied themselves with the education of the people. The administrative posts were transmitted by inheritance in the families of those who held office, and were no longer the prizes of open competition by merit. The period in many respects may be compared to the Middle Ages of Western Europe. Finally during the sixth century before the Christian era, the memory of the ancient institutions was revived by Confucius, who attempted to restore them to his contemporaries. He collected all the authentic documents containing evidences of China's ancient institutions, and from them compiled four special works which have since been universally known as the Book of Odes, the Book of History, the Book of Changes, and the Book of Rites. The four books which this great sage edited, together with the two works written by him, known as the Book of Filial Piety and the Spring and Autumn Annals, and the "Four Books" written by his disciples, became in time the foundation of the moral, historical, and scientific education of the Chinese for many generations.[10] The triumph of the school of Confucianism was, however, not accomplished immediately and without obstacle. In fact, he himself met with little success in attempting to lead the princes of his generation back to the ancient institutions, although after his death several of his disciples succeeded in introducing themselves into the courts of the kingdoms which then divided China. In the middle of the fourth century of the Christian era, Mencius, who like Confucius was born in the eastern part of China, renewed the exhortations of the master, demanded from the kings the re-establishment of higher and lower colleges, and fought strongly against the inheritance of offices, declaring that this abusive practice of handing down public office by heredity was responsible for the disorganization of the government of his time. Mencius also had little success with the princes whom he visited, but he was better heeded by the common people, who were far from satisfied with existing conditions. The new school increased in strength, the number of its followers growing with surprising rapidity, and in spite of the meagre documents which the history of these troubled times offers us, we find that in the middle of

[10] A description of these various works will be found in Giles' Chinese Literature.

the third century before the Christian era there was already a powerful body of men devoted to the cause of education. At this time a prince of the western kingdom of China subjugated all the other kingdoms and became the emperor under the name of Ch'in Shih Huang. We find also that literature containing the doctrine of Confucius was esteemed by the people, and literary men formed a body sufficiently strong to dare to oppose the innovations of the conquerer and urge him to observe the ancient usages described in the classics. Ch'in Shih Huang, who wished that Chinese civilization should date from his reign, rejected these representations and became angry at seeing his edicts constantly criticised in the schools of literary men. In the year 213 B.C., upon the recommendations of his minister Li-ssŭ, he gave the order that all the copies of the works of Confucius scattered through the empire should be burned in order to reduce their tiresome admirers to silence. The decree was executed with vigor and four hundred and sixty literary men, convicted of the crime of having preserved the works of Confucius, were put to death.

It does not follow from what has been said that during the period of decadence there were no schools in China. On the contrary, evidences are not wanting to prove that schools of one kind or another were in existence. The biographers of the great sage Confucius (551-449 B.C.) all agree that Confucius distinguished himself among his fellow pupils, even as a child, and that he studied in school until the age of seventeen, when he was called to the public service. In the later years of his life, he himself established a school on the bank of Chu river, and gathered around him no fewer than three thousand pupils, seventy-two of whom became distinguished scholars, some being later canonized. Again, biographers of Mencius (371-288 B.C.) record that the mother of Mencius once changed her dwelling and went to live in the city, opposite a school, where her sons found examples most worthy of imitation and soon began to profit by them. It appears, however, that although schools of some kind were in existence during the time of these two philosophers, they were no longer conducted under government supervision and financial aid, but had become private enterprises. It was this neglect on the part of the government to maintain the public schools and colleges previously found in districts and departments, as well as in the capital, which led Mencius to make the plea that the government should reestablish the ancient educational institutions and should supervise the instruction given therein.[11]

The period of decadence is thus at the same time a period of transition during which the ancient educational system underwent a radical change. We have seen that during this period a new body of knowledge, as contained in the works of Confucius and his disciples, came into existence to form the basis of the education of later generations and to mark the beginning of influences which made Chinese education purely literary in character and narrowly confined to the study of classics. We have also seen that popular education once supported and supervised by the state became the work of private enterprise and continued thus throughout the ages. But these are by no means the only changes of significance in this period of transition. The epoch is also significant for the birth of numerous philosophers who distinguished themselves for the boldness of their theories and the freedom of their utterance. Among the more important of these philosophers who have exerted an influence upon the development of education, are Confucius, Laotse, Mutse, Yang Chu, Hsun Kuang, and Kwei Ku Tsu. Of these Confucius represents by far the greatest of them all, for this great sage, besides being a philosopher, was also a great moralist and statesman, as well as a matchless teacher. His educational principles and methods together with those of his disciple Mencius are remarkable for their modernity of tone and for their depth of insight into the character and workings of human nature.[12] The moral, social, and political principles embodied in his works and those of his disciples became in time the foundation of the competitive examination system, as well as the content of Chinese education.

In addition to the influence of philosophical schools, one must note a new discovery that had great significance in the development of education, namely, the art of writing Chinese with a brush dipped in ink. This discovery, attributed to a general of Ch'in Shih Huang named Meng T'ien, caused the abandonment of the bamboo tablet and stylus and the general introduction of strips of cloth or silk as materials of writing,

---

11 Mencius, Book I, Chap. I, Art. 13; Chap. V, Art. 14.

12 Cf. Eudem, H: Confucius and his Educational Ideals. *In* Proc. N. E. A., 1893, pp. 308–313; Faber: The Mind of Mencius.

greatly facilitating the communication of ideas and the propagation of general knowledge. No less important than this discovery was the introduction of a new system of writing Chinese characters which was much easier than the one hitherto in existence. These innovations represent successive steps of progress in the art of education. They would have insured for Ch'in Shih Huang a great place in the educational history of China had not his memory been tarnished by the aversion he showed to the school of Confucius and to the literary men who were the devotees of higher education.

It remains to be observed that there is nothing in Chinese history which proves that education, speaking in a broad sense, was totally destroyed under the reign of Ch'in Shih Huang as it is often represented to have been. The acts of the monarch and his ministers, such as the burning of books and the persecution of literary men, represent merely the attempt to suppress a particular school of education and not education as such. It is generally known that Liu Pu Wei, who was the minister of Ch'in Shih Huang until the year 335 B. C., incurred great expense in the search for ancient documents, and composed from them a celebrated collection of works known as Liu Chih Ts'un Ch'iu. Again, we find there was attached to the imperial court a body of scholars known as Po-shih, who had the custody of all the ancient books in the imperial library (Pu-shih-kuan), and were thoroughly familiar with their contents. According to Ma-tuan-lin, Ch'in Shih Huang authorized the study of these ancient books under the direction of the Po-shih, who had many pupils. Furthermore, we are told that he preserved from destruction books on medicine and books of divination, treatises on agriculture and other works which did not contain principles contrary to the established order. What Ch'in Shih Huang and his ministers did, then, was simply to prohibit the literary men from discussing in their schools the merits of the edicts, and it was this discussion that they wished to stop by taking away the ancient books which furnish the basis of comparison and criticism. Nevertheless, it is a sad fact that the ancient system of popular and higher education had passed away beyond return. In order to trace the further development of education we must pass on to the dynasty of Han, which has left an indelible mark upon the civilization of the world, as well as upon the recorded history of China.

CHAPTER III

BRIEF SURVEY OF THE DEVELOPMENT OF EDUCATION UNDER SUBSEQUENT DYNASTIES[1]

(B.C. 206–A.D. 1842)

In the preceding chapter the statement was made that the decadence of the ancient educational system marks the passing of the best educational system China ever had[2]. This is not to be taken to mean that the ancient system is superior to the system of later generations in every detail, for all that is claimed is that the education of early antiquity was better than that of later dynasties in that the former provided popular education at public expense; the training it provided was practical in character and closely related to the life of the times; the school system proper, although forming the only avenue to public office, was in itself sufficient to provide candidates for the purpose; and the different parts of the system were well coordinated, providing a regular promotion from the lowest form of school to the highest. But in many matters regarding the organization of schools, the curriculum, the method of teaching, and many other school problems, the systems of later dynasties were in advance of the ancient educational system. In this survey, however, we can trace only the general trend of development which is necessary to the full appreciation of the development of education in modern times.

Development of Education under the Han Dynasty. *(B.C. 206–A.D. 221)*

One of the remarkable events connected with the Han dynasty was the extended revival of learning which took place soon after the empire had settled down to comparative peace. Liu-

---

[1] The data of this chapter, unless otherwise stated, are derived from the following works: Wen Hsien T'ung K'ao: Sections on School and Examination System, Chiao Yu Shih, Chih Na Chiao Yu Shih, Wan Kuo Chiao Yu Shih; and Biot: Histoire de l'instruction publique en Chine.

[2] See p. 15.

pang, the founder of the dynasty, treated with consideration the literati who were once more commencing to lift up their heads. Upon their incessant demands his successor, Hui-ti revoked in the year 191 A. D. the edict of Ch'in Shih Huang which prohibited the reading of Confucian classics. In the year 136 A. D. a special commission was named to search for manuscripts of these classics with a view to restoring their texts. Great zeal was displayed by scholars in searching for the lost writings. Texts of the Confucian Canon were rescued from hiding-places in which they had been concealed; editing committees were appointed; and great efforts were put forth to repair the injury sustained by literature and education at the hands of Ch'in Shih Huang. The scholars of the day expounded the teachings of Confucius as set forth in these texts; and although their explanations were set aside in the twelfth century when an entirely new set of interpretations became the accepted standard of students, it is due mostly to those early efforts that the Confucian Canon has exercised such a deep and lasting influence over the minds of the Chinese people. In the midst of this great renaissance, the art of making paper from the inner bark of trees was discovered by Tsai Lun. This new invention, together with the art of writing characters with the camel's hair brush discovered under the reign of Ch'in Shih Huang, gave an extra impetus to the new intellectual movement.

Meanwhile, the Confucian principles, or the principles embodied in the Confucian classics, became the state philosophy for the determination of the policy of the government, as well as the standard of the moral and intellectual examinations, which had been re-established for the purpose of selecting men for the service of the government.[3] So great was the respect paid to the Great Sage, that perpetual hereditary rank was conferred upon his senior descendants in the male line, which has continued in unbroken succession down to the present day. This high veneration for Confucius and the principles represented by him had an important bearing upon the subsequent history of Chinese education, for from this time on Chinese education became less liberal than it once was, and the content of education became narrowly confined to the Confucian classics.

---

[3] The establishment of the examination system during the Han dynasty is generally attributed to Wu Wang.

So long as the content of the classics is emphasized, they are effective in molding the lives of the student class; but the moment the form receives the chief attention, as it later did, Confucianism becomes comparable to "Ciceronianism" in the history of European education.

From a larger point of view the over-emphasis upon the teachings of one school of thought to the exclusion of other systems originating during preceding dynasties must be regarded as being extremely unfortunate for the progress of Chinese civilization, for the study of Confucian classics became a habit of the student class who thenceforth held tenaciously to the sayings of ancient sages and were afraid to advance new thoughts of their own. They made no attempt to supersede the civilization of early antiquity, and all they wished was not to fall too far away from it. As a result the thoughts of the scholar class continued to run in the beaten paths of the ancients, and no longer enjoyed the freedom necessary for all true advancement in civilization.

After this brief survey of the general intellectual background of the Han dynasty, we are ready to proceed to inquire into the development of the two phases of the Chinese educational system, namely, the method of selecting men for public office, and the school system. During the Han dynasty, candidates for public office were not all selected from colleges, as they were during the age of Feudalism, the selection being made in various ways at different periods. Sometimes candidates for public office continued to come from colleges; sometimes they were selected and recommended by magistrates and prefects[4]; and not infrequently candidates for higher office were selected from officers holding lower official positions. Local officials were usually given power to select their own assistants and subordinates. Candidates selected and recommended by the magistrate and prefect usually had to submit themselves to an intellectual examination, but under special circumstances they were admitted into office without this examination. During

[4] Under Ch'in Shih Huang a new territorial division was made, according to which China was divided into thirty-six prefectures called chün, each of which had a prefect at its head. Each chün was subdivided into a number of districts called hsien. Each hsien had a magistrate at its head. During the reign of Wu-ti a new unit was created known under the name chou or department, which in size stands between the chün and hsien. In all, twelve chou were created by Wu-ti.

the later Han dynasty, the practice of selecting candidates for office assumed two forms, in one of which candidates were selected by magistrates and recommended by prefects, while in the other they were recommended directly by magistrates to the emperor without the necessity of prefectoral approval. Candidates selected by the second method were usually men of well-recognized ability possessing great reputation. The whole system of selecting men for public office came to be known under the general term Hsüan Chü, but under different reigns it assumed various names, usually derived from the qualifications looked for in the candidates to be selected, such as "Hsien Liang Fang Cheng," meaning "the good and upright"; "Hsiao Lien," meaning "the filial and honest"; and "Po Shih Ti Chih," meaning "learned professors and scholars." It is said that all those who possessed virtue and ability found no difficulty in obtaining office and in making use of the special ability with which they were endowed. So complete was the method used that the system of selecting men for public office has never been surpassed by later generations.

It would be interesting to inquire into the history and method of the various systems used, but such inquiry would carry us far beyond the sphere of our investigation. It is sufficient to note here the important fact that during the Han dynasty colleges no longer formed the only avenue to official life. This accounts for the gradual decadence of public educational institutions, since they were no longer in great need.

The regular reorganization of educational institutions dates from the reign of Wu-ti (140-86 B.C.). Acting under the proposal of a literary man, Tung Chung Shu, who boldly condemned the inheritance of offices, Wu-ti built in his capital, in the year 124 B. C., a college of higher education (Ta Hsüeh) for the training of men capable of filling administrative offices. He also created professors of the five classics (Wu Ching Po Shih) in order to encourage the study of the classics. Local officials were asked to search for men of good morals, well-informed in the knowledge of rituals, and send them to the Ministry of Rites so that they might be appointed pupils of the college. A few years previous to this time, a certain prefect by the name of Wen Wen had organized colleges in his prefecture, created professors, examined the pupils, and encouraged the study of the classics. Wu-ti, having learned of this, ordered that his example be followed and similar efforts be made in other prefectures. During the reign of Kuang Wu, of later Han dynasty, the college was rebuilt; and during the reigns of his successor Ming-ti (A. D. 58–76) and Shun-ti, it was enlarged. By the time of the reigns of Chih-ti and Huan-ti the college had become so flourishing that the number of students was over 30,000. During the reigns of Kuang Wu and his son Ming-ti, China was filled with private schools for higher and lower education. In these institutions students engaged in the study of the classics, in the practice of ritual, and in rendering homage to the memory of Confucius. But finally, in the reign of Huan-ti and his successor Ling-ti, the literary men were once more pushed out of public service through the intrigues of eunuchs and Taoists or followers of Laotze, and under one pretext or another the persecution of scholars was started anew. Education and civil service examinations fell to pieces in the midst of these troubles, and the glorious dynasty of Han came to an end.

Before passing to the next period, it is worth while to note a method of education, similar to the monitorial system of Bell and Lancaster, which was adopted by educators of the Han dynasty, notably Tung Chung Shu, Ma Yung, and Cheng Hsüan. Professors sat in the lecture hall to interpret the meaning of the classics to the most advanced students. These students, in turn, instructed those who were less advanced. The process went on thus till the most immature of the students were reached. In this way the most advanced students had the opportunity of personally listening to the interpretation of the teacher, but the less advanced students were often unable even to see the face of the teacher. It is recorded that Cheng Hsüan was a pupil in the school of Ma Yung for three years, but during all that period he never once saw the teacher's face.

Development of Education from the Han to the T'ang Dynasty. (221–557 A. D.)

The period extending from the close of the Han dynasty to the year 589 was marked by constant wars and internal troubles. China was at first divided into three kingdoms, which were reunited into one single empire under Tsin. Later, after having been invaded in the North by the Tartars, the nation was split into two empires, the North and the South, finally becoming one empire under the Sui dynasty. At the beginning of the West Tsin dynasty, there were created in the capital at least two national schools known as T'ai Hsüeh, or National College, and Kuo Tzŭ Hsüeh, or College for the Sons of the State, which latter had a student body numbering between three to seven thousand; but the invasion of the Tartars from the North soon brought these schools to ruin. During the East Tsin, the national college T'ai Hsüeh was re-established and professors of the classics were appointed, but the instability of the government made their existence precarious. Under the Sung dynasty of the Southern Empire, four colleges of special learning were founded in the capital, namely, Jou Hsüeh, meaning College of Scholars; Hsuan Hsüeh, meaning College of Philosophy; Shih Hsüeh, meaning College of History; and Wen Hsüeh, meaning College of Literature. In addition, there were established in the capital a Kuo Tzŭ Hsüeh, or College for the Sons of the State, and also an academy of graduate scholars called Hsüeh Shih Kuan. These institutions were, however, short-lived. Under the Northern empire, Emperor Tao Wu created in the capital a college with professors of the five classics. Later, Emperor Hsien Wen made provision in each prefecture for two professors of classics, two assistant professors, and sixty students. According to a decree, the number of professors and students was later determined according to the size of the prefecture. The largest prefectures had two professors, four assistant professors, and one hundred students. Those second in size had two professors, two assistant professors, and eighty students. Prefectures of medium size provided for one professor, two assistant professors, and sixty students. The smallest had one professor, one assistant professor, and forty students. Emperor Hsiao Wen established in his capital a college for the Sons of the State and a school for lower education, called Ssŭ Men Siao Hsüeh, meaning small school of four gates. In this way the study of the classics was encouraged, and the scholar class once more began to flourish. Under the Sui dynasty, colleges in the capital and schools in the prefectures and districts were repeatedly brought into existence, and were as frequently closed, with the exception of the T'ai Hsüeh and Kuo Tzŭ Hsüeh,[5] which were in existence for the greater part of the period. The former had only two professors and seventy-two students. There were in existence during this dynasty, however, numerous private schools established by scholars, who, because of their failure to find favor with the government, determined to devote their lives to the pursuit of teaching. Many of these have made themselves famous in history as great educators through their writings and method of teaching, or through their great devotion to education. The most important of these educators are Liu Ch'uo, Liu Hsüan, and Wang T'ung.

The history of education during those three centuries and a half of revolution may be summarized in a few words. The principles of the Confucian classics were not followed regularly in the determination of government policy; and the system of education based on the study of the classics was counteracted by the hostile influence of eunuchs, Taoists, and the followers of Buddhism, which had made great progress in China since the first century of the Christian era. The system of selecting men to fill administrative posts in the government varied likewise in an irregular manner, and the right of selecting and recommending candidates to office was always given to some special officers known as Chung Cheng, who often fulfilled their duty unsatisfactorily. At last all important offices were always given to the sons of high officers, and in time the system of inheriting offices was practically restored.

Development of Education under the T'ang Dynasty. *(620–907 A. D.)*

In the beginning of the seventh century the dynasty of T'ang entered upon its glorious course of three centuries in duration. Under a strong but dissolute ruler immediately preceding, China had once more become a united empire; and although wars and rebellions were not wanting to disturb the even tenor of its way, the general picture presented to us under the new dynasty of the T'ang is one of national peace, prosperity, and progress. This dynasty is usually associated in Chinese minds with much romance of love, with wealth, culture, and refine-

---

[5] Toward the close of the dynasty the name Kuo Tzŭ Hsüeh was changed into Kuo Tzŭ Chien.

ment, with frivolity, extravagance, and dissipation, but most of all with history, literature, and poetry.[6] Under the reign of its first emperors, especially T'ai Tsung, education was fostered and institutions of learning witnessed a rapid development. It was during this period that Japan and Korea, as well as several other neighboring countries, began to send students to China to receive an education.

The system of schools organized during the T'ang dynasty was quite complete. In the Imperial capital there were six colleges, namely, Kuo Tzŭ Hsüeh, T'ai Hsüeh, Ssŭ Men Hsüeh, Lü Hsüeh, Shu Hsüeh, and Suan Hsüeh. Kuo Tzŭ Hsüeh was open to the sons and grandsons of civil and military officials above the third rank and the great grandsons of officials of the second rank. The number of students was limited to three hundred. The T'ai Hsüeh was devoted to the instruction of sons and grandsons of officials above the fifth rank and the great grandsons of the officials of the third rank, the number being limited to five hundred. The Ssŭ Men Hsüeh, meaning college of four gates or four branches of studies, had room for one thousand three hundred students. Five hundred of these places were filled by the sons and grandsons of officials above the seventh rank, and the remaining eight hundred by promising youths of the common people. The Lü Hsüeh, meaning college of law, provided for only fifty students. Shu Hsüeh, meaning the college of calligraphy, had thirty students. Suan Hsüeh, meaning the college of mathematics, also had thirty students. These six colleges all came under the control of Kuo Tzŭ Chien, which was the national university. There were also in the capital two institutions known as Hung Wen Kuan and Chung Wen Kuan, for the education of young nobles and the sons of prime ministers and of officials of great merit possessing the first official rank. In addition to the university and schools for nobles, there was also in the capital one school named Kuang Wen Kuan, established for those who aspired to become pro-

---

[6] "Poetry," says a modern Chinese critic, "came into being with the Odes, developed with the Li Sao, burst forth and reached perfection under the T'angs. Some good work was indeed done under the Han and Wei dynasties; the writers of those days seemed to have material in abundance, but language inadequate to its expression." The complete collection of the poetry of the T'ang dynasty, published in 1707, contains 48,900 poems of all kinds, arranged in 900 books, and filling thirty good-sized volumes. See Giles's Chinese Literature, section on poetry, for further description of the poetry of the T'ang dynasty.

moted scholars or Chin Shih, and also a school called Ching Tu Hsüeh, for the special teaching of the five classics.

Outside of the imperial capital there was maintained a public school in each prefecture, department, and district, as well as in each village. Schools in prefectures of largest and medium size provided accommodations for sixty students; in those of small size they numbered only fifty students. The number of students in the schools of the departments varied from sixty to forty, and that in district schools of various classes ranged from twenty to fifty. In all these public schools as well as in private schools, the five classics of Confucius formed the chief item of the curriculum.

The sections on schools in the Wen Hsien T'ung K'ao of Ma-tuan-lin and those in Yu Han give detailed information concerning the method of teaching and the different works studied in the institutions of the capital, as well as in those of the districts. The same works show the regulation of examinations and the order of promotion of pupils, whether in the same college or from one college to another. They inform us that the prefects sent to the colleges in the capital both the good pupils of their schools and others outside of the school selected by competitive examinations. There were thus two distinct paths by which one could enter the colleges of the imperial court.

The system of selecting candidates for office existing during the T'ang dynasty assumed three forms, namely, Sheng Tu, Kung Chü, and Chih Chü, representing three ways of entering official life. Graduates of the six colleges and two noble schools in the capital and those of departmental and district schools sent to the central government for examination were called Sheng-tu. Non-students sent to the central authority for further examination, after having successfully passed the examination in the district and department, were called Kung Chü. Persons of great ability selected for examination under the personal supervision of the sovereign were called Chih Chü. In other words, there were three avenues by which one could take the examination which led to public service; namely, graduating from the colleges, passing the competitive examination in the district and department, and passing the special examination given by the sovereign. Ma-tuan-lin gives a table of numerous literary degrees instituted by the T'ang dynasty and the conditions of obtaining them. Candidates for the degree of Siu T'sai and Ming Ching had to interpret the meaning of some passages of the classics, and to write a composition on some political subject relative to current events. After the year 680 candidates for the degree of Chin Shih were required to write a piece of poetry, but they were examined less severely than the Siu T'sai upon classics and political questions. Candidates for the degree in law, called Ming Fa, had to analyze some articles on law and passages from imperial decrees. Those for the degree of mathematics, called Ming Suan, were in like manner questioned upon the special treatises of the science of mathematics. However, some of these degrees had only a small number of successful candidates. The degree of Siu T'sai was abandoned in 742 for want of candidates.

The regulations governing the system of schools and the competitive examination established by the early emperors of the T'ang dynasty, as described above, experienced under the reign of their successors some modifications which would be too long to mention in this survey. Toward the year 740 we note the birth of the celebrated Hanlin Yüan or imperial academy attached to the court of the emperor for the explanation of difficult literature. It was this academy which later furnished practically all the imperial historians, inspectors, and directors of public education in the provinces, as well as examiners delegated to preside at the competitive examinations.

In the meantime the scholars were not left in peace; for between the years 730 and 756 the Taoists returned to favor at the court of Hsüan Tsung, who honored their doctrines as much as those of Confucius. In the year 740 the emperor established some colleges named Chung Huan Hsüeh, specially devoted to the study of the works of four great philosophers of the sect of Taoism, namely, Laotze, Chuang Tzŭ, Wen Tzŭ, and Lich Tzŭ. He gave the professors of Taoism a rank equal to that of professors of the imperial college Kuo Tzŭ Hsüeh; he instituted examinations and degrees for Taoism similar to the literary degrees. These innovations did not outlive Hsüan Tsung, for the revolt of a Tartar whom he had protected threw the provinces of the North into the greatest disorder. The imperial capital was ransacked in 759, and it was only in 763 that a new emperor, Tai Tsung, could restore the educational institutions and reorganize the studies upon the foundation laid by his predecessors. Several men attest the fact that the reorganization was poorly effected. The professors of the higher colleges were irregularly paid, and those of the lower colleges were often compelled to till the soil in order to live. Through the influence of the eunuchs, who surrounded Tai Tsung and his weak successors, a number of abuses crept into the examinations of the higher colleges. A decree of the year 807 reorganized the six colleges in the two capitals, western and eastern, Chang An and Lo Yang, but this decree did not do away with the abuses which persisted during the decadence of the T'ang dynasty.

In the year 736 an important change in the control of the competitive examinations took place. The management of the examinations, which up to that time had been entrusted to the Ministry of Civil Offices, was transferred to the Ministry of Rites. The return of this power to the Ministry of Rites was natural enough, since the knowledge of rituals (li) was for centuries the foundation of competitive examination; but as the Ministry of Civil Offices was specially invested with the right of presenting candidates to vacant offices of administration, there resulted from it a perpetual conflict of powers between the ministries. There were thus, on the one hand, the lists of successful candidates from competitive examinations drawn up by the Ministry of Rites, and, on the other, the lists drawn up by the Ministry of Civil Offices selected on the basis of merit. These two administrative departments did not work harmoniously, so that some men chosen by the Ministry of Rites were never admitted to administer public offices, while others whom it had not accepted were invested with positions by the Ministry of Civil Offices. Among those officers appointed without the sanction of the Ministry of Rites were officers of lower rank rewarded for their services; but the majority of them were sons of high officers who could, since the time of Tsin (260–420 A. D.), enter into administrative offices through the influence of their fathers. These sons of officers had, moreover, great facility in entering the imperial college, the natural nursery of high functionaries. The privilege had been defended by the eunuchs since the reign of Tai Tsung, and ever after that time successful candidates in literary examinations encountered no small difficulty in obtaining office. Indeed, so difficult did it afterwards become that among the successful candidates of examinations whose names appeared on the list of the Ministry of Rites, not one in ten succeeded in receiving appointment by the Ministry of Civil Offices. It appears, then, that during the dynasties of Hsia, Shang, Chou, and Han, the selection of scholars and the selection of officers were combined in one system. Scholars who succeeded in passing the examinations were all admitted into public office. But during the T'ang dynasty, the examination of scholars being in the hands of the Ministry of Rites and the appointment of candidates for office in those of the Ministry of Civil Offices, the selection of scholars and of officers became two different things.

Before passing on to the next period, let us note a few more facts connected with the education of this dynasty. Beginning with the eighth century, special calls for men who could enlighten the sovereign were repeatedly made, as under the Han dynasty, and such men were sent to the sovereign by the high officers in the capital and in the prefectures. We find that competitive examinations were instituted for precocious youths and for the selection of officers to be appointed in each prefecture and district to supervise morality. We also find that military examinations were instituted in the year 702 by a decree which determined their tests and degrees, and classified their successful candidates as Ming Ching and Chin Shih. These military examinations were suppressed in the year 800 and re-established in 808. And finally we note that under the same dynasty special schools of medicine were established in the prefectures and districts, and examinations and degrees similar to those for promoted scholars and licentiates were instituted for the encouragement of the study of medicine.

Such in brief was the development of education during the T'ang dynasty, which ended with the year 907. We then pass the stormy reigns of the five dynasties (907–960 A. D.) which contended for China for almost a half century. They present to us no stable educational institutions worthy of consideration. We therefore consider next the great dynasty Sung, which distinguishes itself among all the Chinese dynasties for its unusual zeal for literature and for education.

Development of Education During the Sung Dynasty. (A. D. 960–1280)

With the advent of the Sung dynasty we pass to another period of great intellectual activity. During this period the art of block printing, generally attributed to Feng Tao (881–954), was applied to the production of books and greatly facilitated the spread of knowledge. The departments of history, classical scholarship, general literature, lexicography, and poetry were again filled with enthusiastic workers, eagerly encouraged by a succession of enlightened rulers. And although there was a falling off consequent upon the invasion of the Golden Tartars in 1125–1127, nevertheless the Sungs managed to create a great epoch in the history of Chinese education, and are justly placed in the very first rank among all the builders of Chinese dynasties.

With the accession of T ai Tsu, the founder of this dynasty, the national university in the capital, called Kuo Tzŭ Chien, was restored. It was open to the sons of officials above the seventh rank. The College of Four Gates was re-established in the year 1043 under Jen Tsung; it admitted as students sons of officials as well as those of the common people. In the following year the director of the national university obtained permission to re-establish the T'ai Hsüeh, or national college, which had produced such good results under the dynasties of Han and T'ang. The students were at first poorly lodged for want of sufficient accommodations. By the year 1068, however, the college, having built quarters of suitable dimensions, was able to receive 900 students. The general reorganization of colleges outside the capital also dates from the reign of Jen Tsung, who in 1044 established schools at public expense in all the prefectures and districts. In 1044 the same emperor issued a decree reproaching the officers of the prefectures and departments for not having been careful in the choice of teachers to direct the schools. Later, under the influence of Wang An Shih, a school for the study of law was built near the imperial palace, and a competitive examination for the learned in law (Ming Fa) displaced the examination for the learned in classics (Ming Ching). A military school was also founded and provided with instructors. In the year 1079, a new system, called "Three Halls," was adopted, which classified the students of T'ai Hsüeh into three grades, namely, students of the front hall, students of the rear hall, and students of the upper hall. The number of students of the first class was 2,000, that of the second, 300, and that of the third, 100. The three classes represent three degrees of merit; the students pass by successive examinations from the first to the second, from the second to the third, the last leading directly to administrative offices or to the enjoyment of certain privileges. This system of division and of promotion of students of the national college appears to have been devised to exalt the college and to induce candidates for literary degrees to follow its course of study instead of following the usual method of presenting themselves for the competitive examinations. There were then, as under the T'ang dynasty, two ways of entering official life, one through examination in the colleges, the other through passing the competitive examinations of the provinces. Abandoned in 1086, this system of classifying students into three grades by halls was re-established in 1094, and was kept up for a long time. A decree of the year 1099 extended the system to all the colleges of the empire, and gave to their professors the right to grant degrees of the same rank as those of the competitive examinations of the provinces A decree of the year 1103 suspended even these public examinations. Then the professors, who were no longer appointed by the Ministry of Rites, but by the local prefects, proved themselves to be in general less capable of choosing graduates. Thereupon the scholars made complaints, and in the year 1121 the system of "three halls" was abandoned in the provinces. It was, however, re-established later in 1142 after the emperors Sung had been driven away from their capital by the Chins, and had fixed their residence in Hangchow Fu, the principal city of the present province of Chekiang.

Toward the year 1104 we find mention of schools created by Hui Tsung for instruction in four special sciences: mathematics, medicine, painting, and calligraphy. Ma-tuan-lin and Yu Han have preserved for us the programs of studies followed in these four kinds of schools, which existed at the court and even in the provinces, appearing to have been established in the latter upon the model of the ancient schools of the district, devoted to moral and literary education. But these new institutions had only a precarious existence; they disappeared when

Tsai Ching was driven from the ministry and reappeared when he was recalled. After the invasion of the Tartars, Kao Tsung issued different decrees between the years 1132 and 1145 to reorganize the literary colleges in his new capital and in the provinces which remained loyal to him. A decree of the year 1151 informs us that there were then high inspectors of studies attached to each province as well as each district, and that special lands were appropriated for the maintenance of colleges. But, generally speaking, the resources that were allowed to these institutions in territorial grants or financial subsidy were by no means proportionate to the needs of the great number of students admitted there. The professors no longer had the right to nominate graduates for office and the promotions were made regularly by the path of competitive examinations.

Although the school system did not receive much attention from the first emperors of the Sung dynasty, the system of competitive examination was certainly greatly developed because it was considered useful and necessary for the purpose of obtaining good officers for the state. There was, therefore, besides the practice of recommending candidates by the governors of the provinces, a great variety of higher examinations and of degrees for classics, for law, and other special subjects. The control of these examinations was always in the hands of the Ministry of Rites, which fixed the different conditions of the examination of Chin Shih and other high degrees. The requirements as set forth by Ma-tuan-lin are similar to those of the T'ang dynasty, with the exception that more importance was given to poetry in the examination of Chin Shih. These Chin Shih, or promoted scholars, were thus better prepared to enter the literary work of the Hanlin Academy than to hold offices in the civil administration.

Generally speaking, the scholars of the Sung dynasty were more inclined toward the competitive examination system than toward the colleges, for through the former they could reach administrative positions. It was during this dynasty that the system of examinations was unified, and more stringent rules were adopted to prevent frauds in its management, which rules continued to be maintained until very recent times. We have already observed that toward the close of the eleventh century college professors were given the right to nominate candidates for degrees similar to those given through the competitive examination system, and that a decree of the year 1103 even suspended the system itself. However, after the invasion of the Tartars, professors no longer had the right to nominate candidates for degrees, and promotions were also made entirely through the competitive examination system; but the high importance accorded to poetry in the examinations had altered the original purpose of this institution, so that it furnished few subjects capable of becoming good and honest administrators. The studies had turned away from the aim which Confucius and his early disciples had proposed. "The government," says Ma-tuan-lin, "no longer occupies itself sufficiently to perfect the morality of the people through the knowledge of the ancient rituals (li)."

This survey of the development of education of the Sung dynasty would not be complete without a brief mention of the growth of philosophy which exerted so great an influence over the subsequent history of Chinese education. Ever since the Han dynasty the scholars of China had occupied themselves with the study of the ancient classics, that were restored to them at that time. The work first assumed the form of commenting upon the meaning of the texts, each scholar holding tenaciously to his own views and handing down the same to his pupils. In time these views were held as sacred and no one dared to deviate from them. Special schools of interpretation were thus established. During the later Han dynasty, scholars like Ma Yung, Cheng Hsüan, and others, gathered together the various commentaries, and, having interpreted the classics anew, succeeded in destroying the particular schools themselves. Later, during the T'ang dynasty, the scholars took pains to unify the commentaries of the Han dynasty, often going into great detail. But all the discussions during the Han and T'ang dynasties were confined to the principles of the ancients, and no one dared to search for new truths of universal significance. The work consisted chiefly of committing classics to memory and of writing essays upon them. But during the Sung dynasty, through the influence of Buddhism which had developed in China, a number of great thinkers arose who succeeded in establishing new schools of philosophy, thus changing the educational theory and practice of the T'ang and Han dynasties. To trace their views concerning philosophy and define the province of each does not belong to our present theme. Suffice it to say that most of them were Confucian scholars, but evidences are not wanting to show that their mental activity was stimulated and its direction determined by the speculations of Buddhist and Taoist writers. However, they took care to follow neither, betraying the influence of these sectarians chiefly by the pains taken to steer a middle course between the two. To the one school, mind is the only entity, and matter a deceptive figment of the imagination; to the other, matter is the sole essence, and mind one of its products. Each inculcated a species of monism. The thinkers of the Sung dynasty, combining these one-sided conceptions, boldly asserted a dualism in nature, and fixed on "li and ch'i" force and matter, as the seminal principles of the universe.[7] Those who have made a special study of Chinese philosophy assert that the speculations of the Chinese have in more than one instance anticipated the teachings of modern science, making generalizations which to us appear as among the late results of modern science.

Among the philosophers of this period are the following: Chou Tun I, Shao Yüng, Cheng Hao, Cheng I, Chang Tsai, Liu Chiu Yuan, and Chu Hsi. Of these, the last named exerted the greatest influence over education, and is by far the most celebrated. He was a voluminous writer. In addition to his revision of the history of Ssŭ Ma Kuang, which, under the title of T'ung Chien Kang Mu, is still regarded as the standard history of China, he placed himself in the first rank of all commentators on the Confucian Canon. "He introduced interpretations either wholly or partly at variance with those which had been put forth by the scholars of the Han dynasty and hitherto received as infallible, thus modifying to a certain extent the prevailing standards of political and social morality. His guiding principle was merely one of consistency. He refused to interpret words in a given passage in one sense, and the same words occurring elsewhere in another sense. The effect of this apparently obvious method was magical; and from that date the teachings of Confucius have been universally understood in the way in which Chu Hsi said they ought to be understood."[8]

---

[7] Martin: The Lore of Cathay, p. 37.
[8] Giles: Chinese Civilization, pp. 94–95.

In marked contrast with the philosophers stands the great reformer and economist Wang An Shih (1021–1086) whose public career also exerted a great influence over the development of education during the Sung dynasty. He made a new interpretation of parts of the Confucian Canon in order to justify some of his radical reform measures. He also attempted to reform the examination system, requiring from the candidates not so much grace of style as a wide acquaintance with practical subjects. "Accordingly," says one Chinese author, "even the pupils at the village school threw away their text-books of rhetoric and began to study primers of history, geography, and political economy." "I have been myself," he tells us, "an omnivorous reader of books of all kinds, even, for example, of ancient medical and botanical works. I have, moreover, dipped into treatises on agriculture and on needlework, all of which I have found very profitable in aiding me to seize the great scheme of the great Canon itself." But like many other great men, he was too far in advance of his age. He fell into disfavor at court and was dismissed to a provincial post; and although he was soon recalled, he returned to private life, shortly afterwards to die, though not before he had seen the whole of his policy reversed and his commentary on the great Confucian Canon suppressed.

Before leaving the Sung dynasty we must notice briefly the educational condition among the Liaos and the Chins, two of the Tartar tribes who occupied in turn a portion of the territory in the northern part of China. The Liaos, in imitation of the Sungs in the south, established colleges and examination systems in Liao-tung and other parts of North China. The Chins, who succeeded the Liaos, followed their footsteps in this respect. They restored the competitive examinations in Chinese literature for the selection of men to fill the vacant posts in the conquered provinces. They translated the Chinese classics into their native language, printing them in both Chinese and Chins, and using them in the schools for the education of the children of the conquered race They also held competitive examinations in their own language, and thus at one time gave degrees of Chü Jen and Chin Shih in both Chinese and Chins. Furthermore, they instituted examinations in law and for precocious youths, and also founded numerous colleges of medicine scattered throughout their own kingdom.

The mention of the presence of the Tartars in the north reminds us of one other fact which should not be left unrecorded. The Chinese court in the south in the presence of the Tartar tribes in the north, who were always threatening the rest of China, remembered from time to time that military skill should not be entirely neglected. Thus Kao Tsung in 1135 founded a competitive examination in archery, and in 1157 sanctioned the establishment of a military school in the capital. In 1169 military degrees, similar to the literary degrees, were given in the Chinese army then defending the frontier.

Development of Education under the Yüan or Mongol Dynasty (A. D. 1280-1368)

At the beginning of the thirteenth century, the Mongols appeared upon the scene, and the Chinese formed an alliance with them to attack the kingdom of Chin; but after its downfall, which happened in the year 1235, the Mongols turned their armies against the emperor Sung, who thought that these nomads were returning to their desert homes with their booty. One can easily imagine the distress of the Sung dynasty which made one appeal after another for men to fight in its defense, but finally fell and left the Mongols the peaceful possessors of all China.

The conquerors, who at first showed little taste for the civilization of the Chinese, were not much inclined to give the latter a part in the government, and consequently they were not at all in a hurry to re-establish the competitive examination system and the colleges. However, several of their enlightened rulers were steady patrons of literature and education. Thus, in the year 1269, Kublai, the first Mongol emperor, caused Bashpa, a Tibetan priest, to construct an alphabet for the Mongol language; in 1280 he caused the Chinese calendar to be revised; and in 1287 the national university (Kuo Tzŭ Chien) was opened. Under his sway public schools in the provinces also multiplied. During the reign of Jen Tsung, the examination system was re-established in the capital as well as in the provinces. The candidates were examined by writing essays on the classics and on political subjects As the classics had by that time been translated into the Mongol language, the candidates were divided into two groups, the Mongols having two tests in their own language, the Chinese having three in theirs. As many Chinese as Mongols were admitted to the high civil offices, and in order not to displease the latter the number of offices was immediately doubled in each of the administrative branches. This equal distribution of offices lasted until the ascent of Chun Ti, who suppressed (1335) the literary competitive examinations and gave all the offices to the Mongols. In 1340 the same emperor, in order to appease the discontented of the conquered race, was forced to re-establish the examination system and to maintain it during the remainder of his stormy reign, which terminated with the expulsion of the Mongols into Tartary.

Kublai and his successors encouraged the three sciences which they considered to be useful, namely, medicine, divination, and astronomy. Under their reign China had in all its provinces special schools for the study of these sciences. Regular competitive examinations were open to graduates in medicine who could enter thereby the medical college of the court (T'ai I Yüan), while the graduates of the school of astronomy could, through examination, become assistants in the imperial observatory (Chin T'ien Chien)

When the public school system of the Mongol dynasty was at its best it had two series of schools, one in the capital and the other in the provinces. In the capital there were three national universities (Kuo Tzŭ Chien), one for the Chinese, one for the Mongols, and one for the Mohammedans. In the provinces[9] the following educational institutions were maintained at public expense: a provincial college (Shu Yüan) in each province; a circuit school (Lu Hsüeh) in each circuit; a prefectural school (Fu Hsüeh) in each prefecture; and a district school (Hsien Hsüeh) in each district. In addition, there were also found, in the different circuits, schools for the study of the Mongol language, as well as schools of medicine and of divination. A report dating about the middle of the dynasty gives the number of schools in the country as having reached 24,000. According to the records, however, many of the educational institutions of the Mongol dynasty had merely a nominal existence, and the decrees

[9] Under the Mongol dynasty China was divided into thirteen provinces. This number was increased to fifteen by the Mings, and during the reign of K'ang Hsi, of the Manchu dynasty, a rearrangement of the empire was made by which the number of provinces was increased to eighteen.

of Kublai and his successors were not completely carried out. This state of affairs is due to the fact that, generally speaking, the educational policy of the Mongol dynasty was adopted not from a real desire for education, nor from a firm belief in the importance and efficacy of education, but merely from the desire to please the Chinese in order to gain their confidence and support.

Under such circumstances the Mongol dynasty gave birth to few, if any, educators of reputation and achievement in the history of Chinese education. There is, however, at least one man who will long be remembered for his contribution to education. We refer to Wang Ying Lin, the author of a small primer for school boys known as "Three-Character Classic." For six or seven hundred years this primer was the first book put into the hand of every child throughout the empire. It is an epitome of all knowledge, dealing with philosophy, classical literature, history, biography, and common objects. It has been called a pocket edition of the Mirror of History. Written in lines of three characters each, and being in doggerel, it is easily committed to memory, and every Chinese who has learned to read knows it by heart.

Development of Education under the Ming Dynasty. (A. D. 1368–1644)

As a whole the emperors of the Ming dynasty were liberal patrons of literature and education. T'ai Tsu, the founder of the dynasty, issued during the first years of his reign several decrees to organize the national university (Kuo Tzŭ Chien), the colleges and schools in the provinces, and the examination system. In these decrees he determined the titles of professors, the number of students to be admitted in each kind of college, the subsidy to be given to students, the course of study, the daily program, and the kind of examinations, as well as many other details relating to school organization and management. Being a fond admirer of ancient usages and institutions of learning, he added to the usual classical curriculum the study of military arts and mathematics. He also included military arts and mathematics in the competitive examinations of the province, as well as those of the capital. This plan of combining military and literary studies, however, did not produce very good results, and in the course of a short time the college courses as well as the tests of the examination system became once more purely literary in character. In 1392 he still wished to compel the students of the imperial college to practice archery, and refused to create colleges for the instruction of military men on the ground that he could conceive of only one system of education applicable to all men. A later emperor, Hung Wu, also established schools in the prefectures and districts for the encouragement of education and the training of scholars. During his reign students are said to have been sent to China for education by the governments of Korea, Japan, Siam, and other neighboring countries, and special quarters were provided for them in the imperial college. He also ordered the schools in the provinces to recommend graduates for entrance to the college in the capital. Later, Emperor Yung Lo appointed special officers to supervise education in the provinces and also established military schools in the two capitals of Peking and Nanking and in the garrisons of the frontier. This emperor also succeeded in bringing about the achievement of the most gigantic literary task that the world has ever seen, namely, the compilation of an encyclopedia which contains within the compass of a single work all that had ever been written in the four departments of: 1, the Confucian Canon; 2, history; 3, philosophy; and 4, general literature, including astronomy, geography, cosmogony, medicine, divination, Buddhism, Taoism, handicrafts, and arts.[10]

When the public school system of the Ming dynasty was at its best, it included the following schools: in the capital one national university (Kuo Tzŭ Chien) and a school for the education of young nobles, called Tsung Hsüeh; in the provinces, a

[10] The completed work, on which a small army of scholars—more than two thousand in all—had spent five years, ran to no fewer than 22,877 sections, to which must be added an index occupying 60 sections. The whole was bound up (in Chinese style) in 11,000 volumes, averaging over half an inch in thickness, and measuring one foot eight inches in length by one foot in breadth. Professor Giles calculates that if all these were laid flat one upon another, the column so formed would rise considerably higher than the very top of St. Paul's. Further, each section contains about twenty leaves, making a total of 917,480 pages for the whole work, with a grand total of 366,000,000 words. Taking 100 Chinese words as the equivalent of 130 English, owing to the greater condensation of Chinese literary style, it will be found that even the mighty river of the Encyclopedia Brittanica "shrinks to a rill" when compared with this overwhelming specimen of Chinese industry. Giles: Chinese Civilization, pp. 202–203.

prefectural school (Fu Hsüeh) in each prefecture; a departmental school (Chou Hsüeh) in each department; a district school (Hsien Hsüeh) in each district; and a village school (Shu Hsüeh) in each village. There were also in the provinces a number of schools for the education of the sons of military officers, such as Tu Ssŭ Ju Hsüeh, Tu Chuan Yuen Ssŭ Ju Hsüeh, and Ching Wei Wu Hsüeh.

According to the decree of the year 1368 the national university Kuo Tzŭ Chien was organized in such a way as to take the place of the two ancient colleges, Siao Hsüeh and Ta Hsüeh. Its students included the sons of officers, foreign students, and successful candidates of the competitive examinations in the provinces, as well as students sent from provincial colleges. The university was divided into six departments. The students had to remain there for ten years and had to pass from one department to another through successive examinations of increasing difficulty. Upon leaving the last department they received a degree equal in rank to the degree of licentiates of the competitive examinations of the provinces, and were then permitted to enter the service of the government. As the competitive examinations at first did not furnish a sufficient number of successful candidates, the students of the university did not have much difficulty in obtaining offices in the provinces. Students who had fulfilled certain requirements were placed in the bureaus of the ministries to get experience, and thirty-eight of them were attached to the Hanlin Academy as translators of foreign languages. Beginning with the second half of the 15th century, admission to the bureaus of the ministries was given more or less irregularly. The selection of candidates was made in accordance with the length of time which the student spent in the university instead of the ability shown in the examinations. In this way many of the students who failed to complete the course at the university still were allowed their novitiate in the bureaus.

The colleges and schools in the provinces had four kinds of students, two of which were subsidized and two non-subsidized. The non-subsidized students, according to the edicts promulgated in the years 1426 and 1447, were admitted to the subsidized list if they succeeded in passing certain periodical examinations. From the middle of the 15th century the choice of students for colleges was delegated to special officers who were also responsible for the inspection of colleges and the classification of students into three groups, namely, those qualified to take the competitive examinations for the degree of licentiate, those who ought to continue their studies, and finally those who ought to be punished and dismissed.

The organization of the competitive examinations likewise received some modifications during the Ming dynasty. On several occasions the licentiates who had failed in the competitive examinations for the doctorate (Chin Shih) were called to a second examination less difficult than the first. The number of licentiates admissible in each province was fixed by a decree of 1370; it was successively increased in the different provinces. The number of doctors or Chin Shih to be admitted also became fixed. The candidates of the general competitive examinations were divided into two series of North and South in order to compensate for the inferiority of the candidates of the northern provinces. The separation was removed in 1454. The presidency of the competitive examinations of the province, at first left to local officers, was now delegated to special examiners chosen among the officers of the court and the members of the Hanlin Academy. The general competitive examinations of the imperial capital were presided over by ministers or grand councillors, with the assistance of members of the Hanlin Academy.

The military examinations, which the Mongols regarded as useless, were re-established by the founder of the Ming dynasty. In imitation of the literary examinations, they were divided into provincial examinations and general examinations. They were presided over by the high deputies of the ministry of war. The system, however, was not conducted with much regularity until the year 1506, when it was systematized by a new official program. The examinations included tests in written composition, in archery, and in horsemanship.

The Ming emperors were fairly favorable to the sciences which the Mongols encouraged, namely, medicine, divination, and astronomy. The imperial observatory had a special Department whose members were at first chosen from the country at large; afterwards their offices became hereditary. In a similar way, the vacant places in the Medical Department were generally accorded to the sons of the physicians of the court. Sometimes they were open to competitive examinations, but when that was done the competitors usually came from families which had practiced medicine for generations.

The educational thought at the beginning of the Ming dynasty was, like that of the Mongol dynasty, dominated by the schools of Chu Hsi and the Cheng brothers of the Sung dynasty. Later a new school sprang into existence which was soon able to rival the older school for supremacy and to modify the educational theory and practice of later generations. This new school was founded by Wang Yang Ming, who has been called the "pragmatist before William James." "The thought of Wang Yang Ming contains two cardinal principles: one, the theory that knowledge and practice must not be divorced; the other, that every man should strive to investigate with his individual mind the principles of things in themselves. His practical philosophy is, therefore, a combination of what later became known in the West as Positivism and Pragmatism. Wang Yang Ming stands for individuality in reasoning, for the application of an individual criterion to the phenomena of life. Each mind is to work out its problems on the basis of its own nature; trueness of life and to one's self is what he insisted upon. But the knowledge thus acquired must be subjected to the test of action; only thus can it be proved to have more than a subjective validity. The life of contemplation must be supplemented by the life of action."[11]

The educational principles of Wang Yang Ming, which grew out of his philosophy, are similar to those advocated by Pestalozzi and his followers. He conceives education as harmonious development of the powers of the individual. In order to insure this development the child should be given as much freedom as possible and all restrictions should be removed. To translate his own words: "Child nature enjoys freedom and fears restriction. It may be likened to a plant in its stage of germination; left to itself, it will grow, but interfered with, it will wither and decay. In instructing the child, if his natural inclinations are stimulated, and his innermost self is made happy, there will be no end to his growth. Again, when a plant receives timely rain and the breezes of the spring, then it bestirs itself and begins

[11] Reinsch, Paul S.: Intellectual and Political Currents in the Far East, pp. 133–134.

to grow, but when it suffers hard knocks and frost, then it shrivels and decays. Similarly, when a child is induced to sing songs, it not only enables him to give expression to his ideas and sentiments, but also animates and arouses that which is hidden in the soul. When a child is led to learn rituals, a process which calls for movements of the body, it not only regulates his demeanor, but also helps the circulation of blood and strengthens the body. When he is exhorted to learning, it not only opens up his understanding, but also helps him to express his own thoughts."

Development of Education under the Ching or Manchu Dynasty. (A. D. 1644–1842)

We have now reached the dynasty in which the modern educational movement finds its origin and receives its greatest impetus. Of the ten emperors of this dynasty more than half are known in history as having in one way or another fostered education. Thus T'ai Tsung is known as being responsible for bringing into existence the written Manchu language, and for translating Chinese books into Manchu. He required all the sons of princes and of officers below the age of fifteen to go to school. His successor, Shun Chih, is recorded as having restored the national university (Kuo Tzŭ Chien) and having established schools for the children of the eight bannermen,[13] as well as schools for the education of the sons of nobles. Emperor K'ang Hsi is known as one of the greatest patrons of letters China has ever had. With the aid of the leading scholars of the day, he initiated and carried out several of the greatest literary enterprises recorded in the history of the world. The chief of these are (1) the K'ang Hsi Tzŭ Tien, the great standard dictionary of the Chinese language; (2) the P'ei Wen Yun Fu, a huge concordance of all literature, bound up in forty-four large closely printed volumes; (3) the P'ien Tzŭ Lei P'ien, a similar work, with a different arrangement, bound up in thirty-six large volumes; (4) the Yuan Chien Lei Han, an encyclopedia bound up in forty-four volumes; and (5) the T'u Shu Chi Ch'eng, a profusely illustrated encyclopedia, in 1628 volumes of about 200 pages each. During the reign of this monarch students were received from the

[13] Bannerman is applied to all Manchus in reference to their organization under one or other of eight banners of different color and design.

Liu Chiu Islands and were admitted into the national university under the care of special professors. He also established public schools (Kuan Hsüeh) near the palace, in which courses in reading, writing, and archery were offered. In addition, he encouraged the establishment of village schools (Shu Hsüeh) and public charitable schools (I Hsüeh) in the provinces. Yung Cheng, the successor of K'ang Hsi, also fostered education through the establishment of colleges (Shu Yüan) in the provinces. He himself appropriated 100 taels to each of the provinces toward the building funds. Under his reign Russia sent students to study in the national university under specially designated Chinese and Manchu professors. Chien Lung, who was the grandson of K'ang Hsi, was a worthy rival of his grandfather as a patron of letters and of education. From the long list of works, mostly on a very extensive scale, produced under his supervision, may be mentioned the new and revised editions of the Thirteen Classics of Confucianism and of the Twenty-four Dynastic Histories. In 1772 a search was instituted under imperial orders for all literary works worthy of preservation, and the result was the great descriptive Catalogue of the Imperial Library, containing 3460 works arranged under the four heads of Classics, History, Philosophy, and General Literature, in which all the facts known about each work are set forth, coupled with judicious critical remarks—an achievement which hardly has a parallel in any literature in the world. During the reign of this sovereign, the establishment of provincial colleges was greatly encouraged.

The early emperors of the Manchu dynasty, in assuming the reins of government, left Chinese officials in control of the civil administration, keeping closely to the lines of development which had obtained under the system of the preceding dynasty. The task of providing the new dynasty with an educational system was, therefore, accomplished by accepting as a basis the system of the preceding rulers, and making such changes as were demanded by the spirit of the times. The public school system consisted of three series of schools: 1, schools for nobles (Tsung Hsüeh); 2, national schools (Kuo Hsüeh); and 3, provincial schools (Shêng Hsüeh). Nobles' schools were established in the capital and were of three kinds. One of them, called Tsung Hsüeh, was for the education of the sons of princes and nobles. There were two such schools, one for the Chinese and the other for the Manchus. The age limit of the students was between ten and eighteen. The course included Chinese and Manchu languages, horsemanship, and archery. The second kind, called Chio Lo Hsüeh, was for the education of the sons of certain Manchu nobles, known as Chio Lo. There were eight such schools, one for each banner. Their course of study was similar to that of the Tsung Hsüeh. The third kind, known as the Shengking Tsung She Chueh Lo Kuan Hsüeh, was a combination of the other two schools, specially organized for the education of the nobles and Chio Lo residing in the province of Shengking.' National schools included all forms of schools for the education of the children of the sons of officers, ordinary Manchu Bannermen, and Mongols, as well as the descendants of those Chinese who helped the Manchus to fight against the Mings. They included schools for the teaching of the Mongol and Manchu languages, and also schools for the teaching of mathematics. These schools were found in the provinces of Shengking and Heilungkiang and especially in the capital. At the head of the national schools must be placed the national university (Kuo Tzŭ Chien) which had a well-organized corps of officers and professors. All the offices of this institution were equally divided between the Chinese and Manchus. The students admitted included Bachelors or Siu T'sai, candidates recommended for the examination of the second degree or Kung Sheng, sons of deceased officers of merit or Ing Sheng, students of the imperial academy or Chien Sheng, foreign students, sons of officers of merit, both Chinese and Manchu, and descendants of Confucius and other great sages. The university provided two general courses of study, one classical and the other in government administration. Students taking the classical course were permitted to specialize in one classic or take several classics together. Those who chose the course in government administration were offered the following subjects: Public Rites, Taxation, Laws, Frontier Defence, Waterways, and Mathematics. They were permitted to specialize in one subject or take several subjects at the same time. In addition to the schools already mentioned, we find the existence of other national institutions of an educational character, such as the Hanlin Academy, the Imperial Observatory

(Chin T'ien Chien) and the Imperial Medical Academy (T'ai I Yüan).

Provincial schools maintained by the government included the following: a college (Shu Yüan) in each province, a prefectural school (Fu Hsüeh) in each prefecture, a departmental school (Chou Hsüeh) in each department, a district school (Hsien Hsüeh) in each district, and also village schools (Shu Hsüeh) and charitable schools (I Hsüeh) in cities and villages. Village and charitable schools maintained at public expense were meant for the children of the poor who could not afford to go to private schools. The provincial schools or Shu Yüan were provided for advanced students possessing at least the Siu T'sai degree. The prefectural, departmental, and district schools had four kinds of students, as follows: subsidized students (Ling Shan Sheng), those who made the best record in the annual examination (Cheng Kuang Sheng), those who made the second best record in the annual examination (Fu Hsüeh Sheng), and those who had newly passed the district examination and received the degree of Siu T'sai or Wu Sheng. In all these institutions examinations were held monthly, quarterly, and annuâlly, as well as in special years. Successful candidates from the annual and special examinations were recommended to take examinations for higher degrees. At the beginning of the modern period these provincial schools were in a stage of decadence. In most of them professors and students had merely a nominal existence. No regular classes were conducted in these schools, and all that was required of the students was to appear at the periodical examinations. This state of affairs was brought about through the discovery on the part of the students that their promotion was dependent upon examinations given by the director of studies on his tour of inspection, and not upon their attendance in the school. Consequently they went to school only when the director was making his visits and giving his examinations and remained at home during the rest of the time. Thus the education of provincial schools was ruined by the system of inspection and of periodical examinations.

The gradual decadence of the school system was counterbalanced by the growing importance of the competitive examination system, which had by this time developed into a colossal machine, with ramifications extending to every nook and corner of the great country. True it is that during the Manchu dynasty entrance to official life might be gained through the purchase of rank, through recommendation of higher officers, and through special appointment by the sovereign; yet it is also true that the competitive examination continued to be the method used to ascertain the qualifications of candidates for government employment. Since the mode of operation of this system as we find it at the beginning of the modern period is not an unfamiliar, though by no means an exhausted, subject, we shall merely enumerate the successive examinations which constituted the rungs of the ladder leading to the official life:

1. Matriculation examination in the districts and prefectures.
2. Examination for the first degree, Siu T'sai, which takes place in the chief city of the district.
3. Provincial examination for the second degree, Chü Jen, held in the capital of the province under the supervision of the literary chancellor. It is open to those possessing the first degree.
4. National examination, held every three years in the capital for those possessing the second degree. Successful candidates for this examination are given the degree of Chin Shih.
5. Palace examination, open to those possessing the degree of Chin Shih. Successful candidates become members of the Hanlin Academy.
6. Examination in the presence of the emperor. It is open to those possessing at least the second degree. Successful candidates after having been given official rank are admitted into public service.

The educational situation in China at the beginning of the modern era can be stated in a few words. Higher education is fostered by the government, but rather as a means to an end than for its own sake. The great end is the repose of the state; the instruments for securing it are able officers, and education is the means for preparing them for the discharge of their duties. An adequate supply of trained candidates once secured, the education of the people ceases to be an object, although theoretically the importance of education as moral training is not only still recognized but often emphasized. This attitude of the government is reflected in the attitude of the people. To many of them education has come to mean nothing more than preparation for official life. Those who have no ambition to enter the official career regard as unnecessary all intellectual effort beyond the securing of a training for business and daily life. The kind of educational institutions found in the country also seems to support this conclusion. Most of the schools in the capital are intended for the education of nobles and other privileged classes. In the provinces schools have merely a nominal existence, and, at their best, are intended only for the most promising of the student class. There is nothing approaching a system of common schools maintained by the state and designed to diffuse among the masses the blessings of a popular education. Indeed, it may be said that popular education is almost entirely left to private enterprise and public charity, the government contenting itself with gathering the choicest fruits and encouraging their production by rewards in the way of degrees, official titles, and other public recognition. Such in brief is the condition of public education in China on the eve of a new educational era.

CHAPTER IV

TRANSITION FROM TRADITIONAL TO MODERN EDUCATION

(A. D. 1842–1905)

Beginnings of Modern Schools

The beginning of modern schools may be said to date from 1842, the year which marks the opening of the five Chinese ports to foreign trade and commerce. The pioneers of the movement were the missionaries who had been waiting at the door for an opportunity to come into China. They lost no time in establishing schools as an instrument for the dissemination of Christian knowledge and faith. The schools thus founded, though not strictly confined to the children of the Christians, remained chiefly as the place where new converts were educated and preserved from too intimate contact with the unbelieving world. At all events the work of those pioneer missionaries did not have the scope and character which it has assumed in recent years. They had no well-established educational policy. Each school was opened as the exigency of the occasion demanded and the funds of the home board permitted. Their schools were, moreover, confined to the children of the humbler classes. The few who acquired a western education therein had little prospect of employment in the government. In spite of these and other shortcomings, it must be admitted that for some time the schools of the missionaries were practically the only institutions where some form of modern knowledge was taught and for this reason they may justly claim to have been the first modern educational institutions in China.

The treaty of Tientsin, ratified in 1860, called into being the Tsungli Yamen or Foreign Office. With its establishment there was at once felt an urgent need of men familiar with both the written and the spoken languages of the several treaty Powers, in order to carry on diplomatic relations with them. To be sure, the treaty in question contains a clause requiring that all despatches should be accompanied by a Chinese translation, but this arrangement was to last only for a period of three years, and was made to allow the Chinese government time to provide her own interpreters. In order to meet this demand, the government established, in 1862, through the recommendation of the Tsungli Yamen, a school in Peking, until recently known as the T'ung Wen Kuan, for the training of official interpreters.[1] This school, though connected with the Foreign Office, was placed under the direction of the late Sir Robert Hart who was then Inspector General of Maritime Customs. In 1866 it was raised to the rank of a college. Before that time only foreign languages were taught; then a scientific department was added. In 1868 Dr. W. A. P. Martin was called to the professorship of international law, and in 1869 he was appointed the first president of the college.

Soon after the establishment of the T'ung Wen Kuan, the Tsungli Yamen established two auxiliary schools, one of which was located at Shanghai and the other at Canton. At different times graduates of these schools were sent to the T'ung Wen Kuan at Peking for further study, the latter being the higher school and offering a more advanced course of study. As the years went by and occasion demanded, departments of foreign languages, such as English, French, Russian, and Japanese, were added one after another to these schools.

Besides the T'ung Wen Kuan and its auxiliary schools, several other institutions of learning came into existence and these in turn became the forerunners of the modern school system. In 1867 Viceroy Tseng Kuo Fan, through the persuasion of Yung Wing, established a mechanical school as an annex to the Kiangnan Arsenal at Shanghai in order to teach the theory as well as the practice of mechanical engineering, with a view to enabling China in time to dispense with the employment of foreign mechanical engineers and machinists, and thus to be perfectly independent. In the same year two naval schools, one French and the other English, were established in Foochow. The Northern Government Telegraph College was established at Tientsin in the year 1879. In 1887 Li Hung Chang formulated

[1] The T'ung Wen Kuan was in 1903 amalgamated with another school known as I Hsüeh Kuan (school of the science of translation).

the plan of establishing a university at Tientsin. With funds contributed by both Chinese and Europeans a spacious building was constructed. Dr. Charles D. Tenny was called to the presidency of the proposed university, but for some reason no further steps were taken to carry out the plan until after the war with Japan. In 1890 the Chinese Imperial Naval College was established at Nanking, and two years later the government Mining and Engineering College of the Hupeh Board of Mines was established at Wuchang. One year later, in 1893, the medical college for the army was established in Tientsin. At Wuchang Viceroy Chang Chih Tung also attempted to institute reforms by introducing western education. Colleges of agriculture, languages, mechanics, mining, and military science were organized. Professors were invited from America, Belgium, England, Germany, and Russia.

Early Attempts to Modernize the Examination System

Meanwhile, attempts were made to introduce reforms in the time-honored examination system itself. As early as the year 1869 the viceroy of the Fukien province memorialized the throne suggesting that a knowledge ot mathematics should be required of candidates competing for degrees in the examinations. In 1875 Li Hung Chang, then viceroy of Chili, presented a similar memorial recommending the introduction of physical science as well as mathematics among the subjects of examination. Both of these recommendations, however, failed to receive the royal sanction, showing that the time was not yet ripe for the change. But while the central government was so reluctant to modify the examination system, the new learning was all the time gaining in popularity with the more progressive literati of the country. Finally, in 1887, two years after the close of the war with France, the government, now fully convinced of the necessity of reforming the educational system, decreed that mathematics and science be introduced in the government examinations, and for the first time in Chinese history modern sciences were placed on a par with classical learning. This official recognition of the parity between science and linguistics, indicating the coming victory of realism over humanism, is remarkable in that it preceded similar events in most of the modern nations; for example, this did not happen in Germany until the adoption of the reform program of 1901, and in France not until the adoption of the reform program of 1902. Owing to the fact, however, that the literary chancellors who presided over the examinations were themselves unfamiliar with the new subjects, very little was actually accomplished in the way of modifying the old stereotyped classical examinations. Nevertheless, the step taken was of great significance, and its importance in the history of Chinese education cannot be overestimated. A writer of the time, commenting upon the reform thus introduced, remarks that the thin edge of the wedge has been driven into the competitive examination system which in the end will rive asunder the old wall of Chinese conservatism, liberalizing the minds of the literati and setting them forward in the path of progress and reform.

Educational Commissions to Western Countries

The educational commissions of this early period played no less important part in the development of modern education in China. One of these commissions was brought about by the late Dr. Yung Wing, who was a Chinese graduate of Yale College.[2] In 1868 he proposed to the high authorities in China a scheme for sending picked students to America to be thoroughly educated for government service. As an experiment one hundred and twenty students were to be selected and divided into four groups of thirty students each, one group to be sent out each year. They were to have fifteen years to finish their education. Their average age was to be from twelve to fourteen years. If the first and second years' work proved to be successful, the scheme was to be continued indefinitely. Chinese teachers were to be provided to keep up their knowledge of Chinese while in the United States. Over the whole enterprise two commissioners were to be appointed, and the government was to appropriate a certain percentage of the Shanghai customs revenue to maintain the mission. Largely through the influence of Tseng Kuo Fan, Ting Yi Chang, and others high in authority, the scheme received the sanction of the emperor soon after the Tientsin massacre (1870) and Yung Wing and Chin Lan Pin, the latter a member of the Hanlin Academy, were

[2] Cf. Yung Wing: My Life in China and America.

appointed to take charge of the newly created commission. In 1871 a preparatory school for the training of students to be sent abroad was established in Shanghai under the supervision of Liu Kai Sing, who for a number of years was one of the secretaries of Viceroy Tseng Kuo Fan. In the latter part of the summer of 1872, the first thirty students were sent over to the United States, and by the fall of 1875 the last group of students had arrived in America. The youths were distributed by twos or by fours in New England families, where they were cared for and instructed until they were able to join classes in graded schools. In course of time, they proved themselves almost without exception to be capable and active in the tasks set before them, and as their hold upon the English language increased, they began even to outrank the brightest of their American classmates. The Commission made its permanent headquarters in Hartford, Connecticut, where, at the recommendation of the commission, and with the approval of Li Hung Chang, who had assumed charge of the Commission upon the death of Tseng Kuo Fan, a handsome and substantial building was erected in 1874 and occupied at the beginning of the following year.

To the great disappointment of the thoughtful men of the time, the scheme, so auspiciously inaugurated, did not live long. The complexion of this educational enterprise began to change with the installation of Wu Tzŭ Tung as head of the Commission in 1876. No sooner was this man placed in office than he began to make misrepresentations to the Chinese government regarding the intellectual and moral character of the students and the general result of the Commission. These false reports continued for some time till a censor from the ranks of the reactionary party came forward and, taking advantage of the strong anti-Chinese prejudice in America, memorialized the government to break up the mission and have all the students recalled. This proved the death-knell of the enterprise, for in 1881 we see the actual break-up of the Commission and the recall of all the students, numbering one hundred in all. The real motive which prompted the government to withdraw the students when they were about to gather in the most important advantages from their studies, and the humiliations to which these young students were subjected upon their return to the land of their birth, form an interesting chapter in the history of modern education in China.

A less known but no less important educational enterprise was undertaken by the Foochow Arsenal. In 1876 it sent forty-six students abroad to study ship-building and navigation. These students met a better fate than those of the other mission, although even they did not receive so warm a welcome upon their return as they deserved. It must be remembered, however, that these schemes of sending students abroad can in no wise be considered failures, for with the passing of years a larger and larger number of those pioneer students have become men of influence in the promotion of progress and reform in their native land. Indeed, not a few of them have risen to positions of great impo tance and have achieved sufficient distinction to prove their worthiness of the effort bestowed upon them, thus going far toward justifying the educational experiment which is now being repeated on a much larger scale.

Effect of the Chino-Japanese War upon Educational Reform

The disastrous war with Japan (1894–1895) and the general foreign aggression which followed it, humiliating though they were to the national honor of China, gave a new impetus to the cause of educational reform. Many people were convinced for the first time that further reforms in education were necessary in order to place China upon a firmer basis. This conviction became so prevalent that many of the literary men, some of whom were quite advanced in age, sought western learning by attending missionary schools and colleges, by employing private tutors, by forming reform clubs, and by reading such translations of western books as were available. The emperor, Kuang Hsü, himself became so interested in western science and learning that he ordered his eunuchs to search out and bring to him all the translations of books on western learning that could be found. The demand for the new learning became so great that by 1896 all schools where western language and science were taught were overcrowded with pupils. Even young and inexperienced students found it easy to obtain lucrative positions as private teachers. In the midst of this zeal for western learning, several important institutions came into existence. Two of these need special mention: One is the university in Tientsin, now known as the Peiyang University. The real beginning of this institution dates as early as 1887, but the actual organization of the university did not take place until after the war with Japan, when arrangements were made to finance the institution with funds from the telegraph administration, the China Merchants Steamship Navigation Company, and the Office of the Superintendent of Customs or the Taotai's Yamen. The other important educational institution is the Nanyang College, which was established in Shanghai in 1897, mainly through the influence of Sheng Hsüan Huai. Both of these institutions, although their character has been changed considerably since their first establishment, have, nevertheless, withstood all the political storms which have been raging over China during the last fifteen years, and are now ranked as among the best of the institutions for higher learning which China possesses.

The Book of Chang Chih Tung and his Recommendations Concerning Educational Reform

Soon after the war with Japan, Chang Chih Tung, then viceroy of the Hupeh and Hunan provinces, published a remarkable book known as Ch'uan Hsüeh P'ien or An Exhortation to Learning.[2] In this now famous book the viceroy advocated the establishment of modern schools in every province, circuit, prefecture, department, and district. He outlined a system of schools as follows: universities in the provincial capitals and at Peking, colleges in the prefectural cities, and high schools in the districts, all planned out on a graded system, with the lower institutions co-ordinated with the higher ones. The curriculum of the high schools was to be the "Four Books," Chinese geography and history (abridged), arithmetic, geometry, and the elements of science; that of colleges, the higher branches of science, the "Five Classics," the T'ung Chien (a history), government, foreign languages and literatures; and the curriculum of the universities was to include subjects of still higher grade. One of the ways of putting his scheme into practice which he suggested was to convert temples and monasteries of the Buddhists and Taoists into schools, and to appropriate temple

---

[2] The book has been translated into English by Samuel I. Woodbridge and is known under the title "China's Only Hope."

lands and incomes for educational purposes. The courageous viceroy also urged the necessity of abolishing the use of the so-called "eight-legged essay"[4] in the examinations and of making the new learning the test of scholarship through the introduction into the examinations of practical subjects, such as history, geography, and Chinese government, in addition to the commonly used classics.

The book, dealing with issues so live and so exciting and coming from the pen of one so influential both in action and in intellect, naturally attracted much attention. By the order of the emperor it was handed to the Grand Council of the State and copies of it were distributed to the viceroys, governors, and literary examiners of China in order that it might be extensively published and widely circulated in the provinces. As a result the book was devoured with the greatest avidity by the scholars throughout the country, and so enthusiastic was the reception accorded to it that within a short time millions of copies were distributed. In this way the seed of a far-reaching intellectual awakening was scattered broadcast in the minds of the people, preparing them for reform measures even more drastic and radical than those already introduced.

Reforms and Counter-Reforms of 1898

In the memorable year of 1898 the young emperor Kuang Hsü, backed by a host of reformers, including the well-known K'ang Yu Wei and Liang Chi Chao, issued a series of decrees in which were embodied some of the most sweeping reforms China has ever known.[5] The reforms introduced include the establishment of a system of modern schools, the abolition of the "eight-legged essay" in the examinations, the introduction of short, practical essays upon subjects suitable to modern needs and conditions, and the sending of young Manchus abroad for a western education. These innovations and others touching upon the reform of the military examination system, the encouragement of the translation of foreign books, and the establishment of newspapers, literally shook the empire from

---

4 These essays were so called because they were divided into eight heads in an artificial manner. The style was stilted, sentences of four or six characters alternated, and each set of ten characters had to be antithetical.

5 Cf. Emperor Kuang Hsü's Reform Decrees, 1898. Reprinted from the *North China Daily News*.

one end to another. For a time the reform movement promised to become national in character and its spirit to permeate the provinces and to move the minds of the great nation.

But unfortunately a reactionary movement as radical and drastic as that of reform, arose and finally gained full sway. At the back of the reform movement was a small band of earnest men whose excessive zeal led to premature action. A plot was conceived, under which the Empress Dowager was to be arrested and imprisoned; but this being made known to that resourceful woman, she turned the tables by suddenly arresting and imprisoning the Emperor, and promptly decapitating all the conspirators, with the exception of a few who succeeded in making their escape. All prospect of reform now disappeared from the imperial program; the edicts which had raised premature hope in this direction were annulled and the old regime was to prevail once more. All newspapers were suppressed; schools projected in prefectural, sub-prefectural, and district cities were held in abeyance; the right to use temples, monasteries, and nunneries for school purposes was revoked; and the use of the eight-legged essay in the examinations and the old order of conducting military examinations were once more restored. Of all the educational reforms of that year, the imperial university alone withstood the storm of reaction.

Effect of the Boxer and the Russo-Japanese War upon the Progress of Modern Education

The retrograde policy of which we have been speaking lasted till 1900, when the Boxer outbreak once more changed the state of things. During those days of storm and fury almost all of the modern schools and colleges in northern China were temporarily abandoned; some of them, including the Peiyang University, were even completely destroyed. Fortunately the outbreak, through the refusal of the viceroys in the southern provinces to join the movement, was confined to the North, else the same sad fate would have befallen the schools in the South. But although the immediate effect of the political uprising was detrimental to the cause of the new learning, its ultimate influence was helpful; for after China had been humbled and peace once more restored, the program of educational reform was again adopted and the Empress Dowager, having learned a dearly bought lesson, began to advocate the very measures she had so vigorously resisted only a short time before. She not only re-enacted many of Kuang Hsü's edicts, but made the influence of some of them even more far-reaching than before. From this time on modern education progressed by leaps and bounds.

Among the immediate results of the Boxer uprising was the establishment of the Shantung Provincial College with Dr. W. M. Hayes as its president, and the University of Shansi with Dr. Timothy Richard at its head. The latter institution has a singular history. During the Boxer uprising a number of missionaries were killed in the province of Shansi. When the trouble was over, compensation was demanded by the Powers both for the buildings that were destroyed, and for the missionaries that were killed. A certain number ot the missionary bodies refused absolutely to take any compensation. Animated by the spirit of the early Christian church, they were not willing that the blood which had been shed for the sacred cause should be paid for in money. At this juncture a deadlock was threatened. The western governments were insisting on compensation, but were uncertain as to how that compensation should be made. At this crisis, the Chinese authorities in charge of the matter sent for Dr. Timothy Richard, one of the Protestant missionaries in whom they had confidence, to help them settle the case. Thereupon Dr. Richard made a recommendation which appealed at once to all parties concerned, namely, that the money should be devoted to the founding of a great university in Shansi. Under such peculiar terms the university was founded. It was under the government of China, and yet not completely so, for according to the terms of arrangement, Dr. Richard was to have the control of the western side of the education at least for ten years. At the end of that period it was to return to the ordinary status of a government university.[6]

In the midst of attractive promises of reform came the Russo-Japanese War, with all its surprises. Among the causes to which the Manchu court ascribed the success of the Japanese, western learning took a high rank, and this led to renewed efforts and

---

6 Cf. Gascoyne-Cecil: Changing China, pp. 274–275.

more firm determination to carry out the reform policy. The cry of the time was that what Japan has done, China by adopting similar reforms and taking similar steps can and will do. Indeed, so astounded were the Chinese by the prowess displayed by Japan that many were willing to sit at the feet of the Japanese, their one-time pupils, in order to learn the secret of success. For a time students poured into the island empire and Tokio became the Mecca of western learning to the Chinese. It is estimated that the number of Chinese students in Japan reached as many as 15,000. In the course of a few years returned students from Japan were found throughout the length and breadth of the great country taking an active part in the cause of progress and reform. Those who remained in Japan devoted a large part of their time to the editing of magazines and the translation of books, a veritable flood of literature thus pouring back to their fatherland, and reaching every nook and corner of the empire. Some of this literature, flowing from the pens of young men flushed with the new learning and burning with patriotism, was naturally somewhat violent in tone and made sensational reading, but it produced its effect on the people, who needed something unusual to wake them out of their lethargy.

Recognition by the Government of the Graduates of Modern Schools

Another important and far-seeing step in the educational reform was taken when Yüan Shih Kai recommended to the throne that some form of official recognition be given to the graduates of modern schools as it was given to the successful candidates of the competitive examinations. On December fifth of that eventful year, 1901, a decree was promulgated according to which the new learning was given proper recognition.[7] The provisions of this decree are as follows: "Graduates of the lower schools of promise and ability are to be sent to the middle schools to complete a course of higher studies, and graduates from the latter selected for their talents and ability are to be sent to the colleges of their native provinces to go through another course of study. After these have graduated from their respective colleges they are to be styled "students of the superior class."

[7] Cf. King, H. E.: The Educational System of China as Recently Reconstructed, p. 32; and Lewis, R. E.: The Educational Conquest of the Far East, p. 181.

They are then to be thoroughly examined by their own viceroys or governors and literary chancellors and the most promising are to be granted passports to go to Peking for re-examination at the Peking University, after which they are to await an imperial decree bestowing upon them the literary degrees of Chü Jen or Promoted Scholar, and Kung Shen or Senior Licentiate. The latter are then to remain and again compete at the next examinations for the said Chü Jen degree. Those who have obtained their Chü Jen degree are again to undergo another strict examination at the Peking University, and the most promising are to be sent by the said university authorities to the Board of Rites. The said board will then memorialize the Throne asking that some high Ministers of the Court be appointed to hold a special examination of these Chü Jen candidates and a recommendation will then be presented to the Throne asking for the granting of the Chin Shih or Doctor's degree to the successful students. An examination of the latter will then be held in one of the throne halls, after which the successful candidates are to be introduced to the Throne, when the grade of Hanlin, or Secretary of the Six Boards, or Secretary of the Grand Secretariat will be bestowed upon them.

Effort to Modernize the Traditional Schools

One of the educational reforms was the attempt to modernize the traditional schools. Here is a notable instance. In 1901 a memorial was presented to the Throne by Sun Chia Nan, the President of the Hanlin Academy, in which he made known the fact that the members of the said academy, instead of studying such subjects as would prepare them for appointments in diplomatic, consular, and other departments of the government service, spent their time in trivial occupations, such as composing poetry, which were perfectly useless for the needs of the time. He suggested that they be required to devote themselves to the study of the principles of government, mathematics, chemistry, and other special subjects which they might desire to study. The memorialist further recommended that the members of the academy be allowed to enter the Peiyang University or Nanyang College for a course of training if they were so inclined. The memorial in question was approved and Sun Chia Nan was ordered to draw up a list of subjects to be pursued by the members of the academy. In 1902 a decree was issued commanding the members of the Academy to study diligently ancient and modern history, politics, and western learning, with a view to preparing themselves to render service to the government. The chancellor of the academy was ordered to examine the progress of their studies every five months and report the results to the Throne.

New Provisions for the Encouragement of Study Abroad

In the meantime the experiment of sending students abroad was resumed on a much larger scale. In 1901 a decree was issued by the Empress Dowager commanding her diplomatic representatives abroad to search for those Chinese youths who had shown special talent while studying in the schools and colleges in foreign countries, those who had graduated with honor, and those who possessed diplomas in their various professions. Such men were to be sent to China to undergo an examination, and upon the basis of merit shown in the examination proper degrees were to be conferred upon them. Later in the year another edict was issued in which the viceroys and governors throughout the country were asked to follow the good example of viceroys Liu K'un I, Chang Chih Tung, and Kwei Chun by sending young men of scholastic promise abroad to study those branches of western science or art best suited to their abilities and tastes, so that in time they might return to China and place the fruits of their knowledge at the service of the country. The same edict made special provision regarding the giving of official recognition to returned students and the financial support of the students. A Chinese student returning from abroad with his diploma proving the completion of his studies could present himself before the viceroy or the governor and the literary chancellor of his native province for examination, and if found satisfactory he would be recommended to the Ministry of Foreign Affairs for appointment. The expenses of the students while studying abroad were to be paid by the provinces to which they belonged. Any student desiring to go abroad to study at his own expense could obtain an official dispatch from the viceroy or governor of his province introducing him to the Chinese minister accredited to the country where he wished to obtain his education and requesting the minister to take care of him and render him any needful help. Private students, if they so desired, could have the same privileges accorded to those sent under government expense, and, like the government students, would be granted literary degrees of the proper kind, should they be able to meet the required tests.

Shortly after the proclamation of the above decrees, an important memorial signed by Chang Chih Tung, Chang Pai Hsi, and Jung Ching, was presented to the Throne, in which the memorialists declared that the sending of young and inexperienced students to foreign countries had not been altogether a success, and recommended that older and better educated men, such as Hanlins and princes of high rank, be sent abroad so that the country might receive more benefit from their experience and study. As a means of encouragement they proposed the following scheme of reward based on the length of time spent abroad: first class reward to those who spent at least three years in foreign countries, second class to those who spent at least two years in Europe and America; and third class for those who traveled in Japan over one year. In addition to the special reward, all officials traveling abroad were to receive their regular salary. The object of sending such men abroad was to examine the methods of foreign government, especially their diplomatic policy, their military and naval regulations, and their educational systems. Those who traveled abroad were expected to take notes of their observations, which upon their return to China were to be handed to an imperial inspector and rewards were to be given only to those who had made valuable notes.

In 1905 another edict relative to sending students abroad was issued, which throws further light upon the attitude of the government toward the education of students in foreign countries. In this decree the Throne expressed its deepest pleasure at the fact that the viceroys and governors had obeyed the command to send students abroad, and suggested that since there were already many Chinese students in Japan a large number should now be sent to Europe and America. Highest commendation was given to those who were willing to cross the wide ocean in order to gain substantial knowledge for the benefit of their mother country. The ministers abroad were asked to take special care of the students under their charge and to treat them like their own children and relatives. They were also asked to see that students lived orderly lives and were diligent in their studies. In case any student should be found to be ill or in want of money to prosecute his studies, the ministers were expected to give him pecuniary and other necessary assistance. The decree concluded by exhorting the government officials, on one hand, not to look slightingly on such students, but to assist the Throne in every way to raise up men of ability for the betterment of the country; and by reminding the students, on the other hand, of the importance of their mission and urging them to choose those subjects of study for which they were best fitted, so that upon their return they might be qualified to shoulder positions of responsibility.

The First Modern School System

The matter of establishing a modern school system upon a national basis was taken up with all seriousness. During 1901 an edict was issued commanding that all provincial colleges (Shu Yüan) in the capital cities of provinces be turned into modern universities or colleges modeled after the Imperial University at Peking; that middle schools be established in every prefecture and department; that elementary (higher primary) schools be established in every district, and lower primary schools in the country at large. The course of study was to include Chinese classics, history, principles of government, and western sciences. In 1903 a special commission, consisting of Sun Chia Nan, Chang Pai Hsi, and Chang Chih Tung, was appointed to draw up a detailed plan for a national public school system. The report of the Commission, including regulations as to discipline and curricula, and suggestions as to the method of establishing schools, when printed consisted of four volumes. Receiving the sanction of the imperial government, this plan became the authorized program for educational changes throughout the empire.

The following chart embodies the system of education proposed by the Commission:

FIRST MODERN EDUCATIONAL SYSTEM
1903

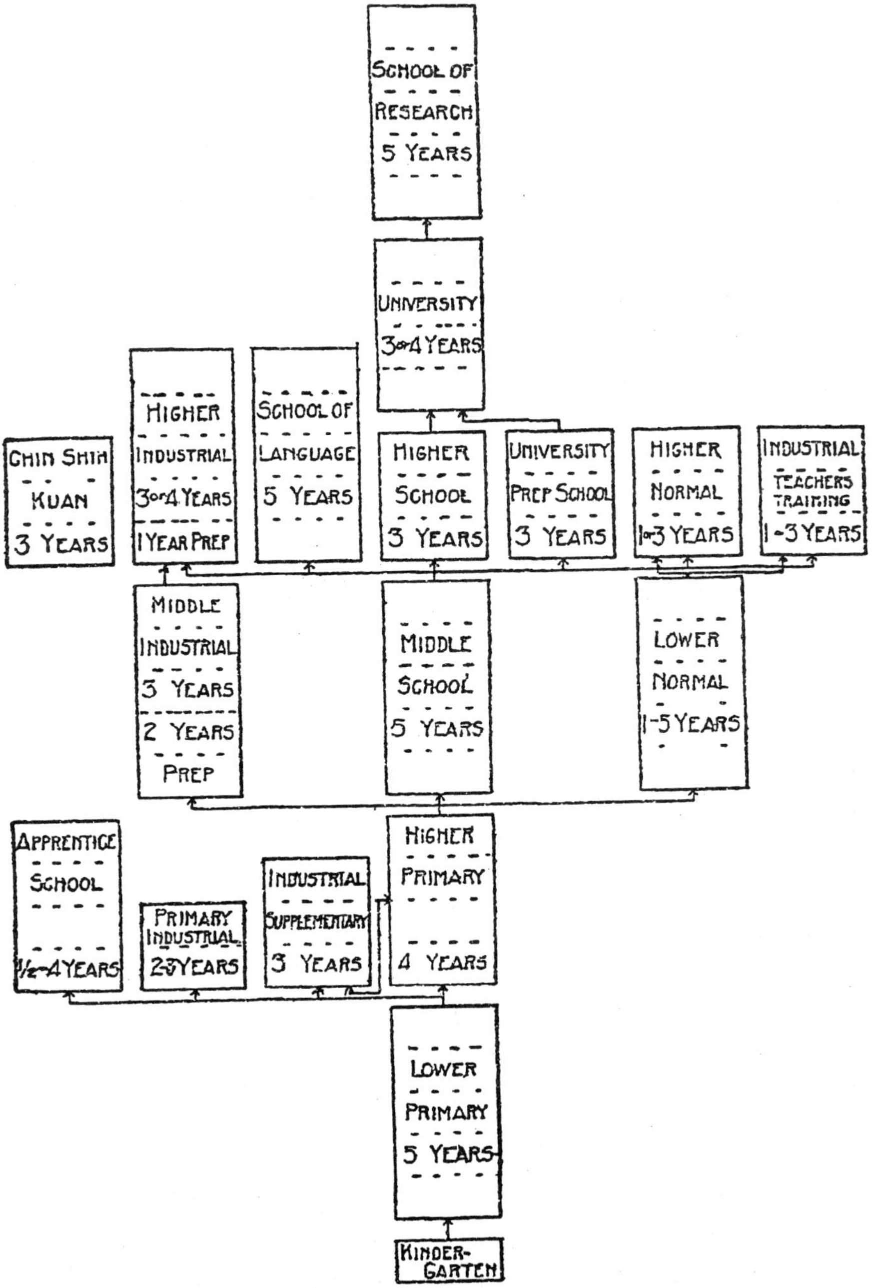

N. B. Industrial supplementary schools also admit those already in industrial pursuits.

Kindergarten

Kindergartens are designed for the care and instruction of children between three and seven years of age. They are established in or near the existing orphanages and "homes of virtuous widows" in the various districts. Children are allowed to remain in the kindergarten not longer than four hours a day. Tuition is free.

Lower Primary School

The aim of the lower primary school is to give to children above seven years of age the knowledge necessary for life, to establish in them the foundation of morality and patriotism, and to promote their physical welfare. The government is to establish model schools, at least two in each small district, three in each large district, and one in each large village. The curriculum includes the following eight subjects of study: morals, Chinese classics, Chinese language, mathematics, history, geography, nature study, and physical culture. Drawing, hand work, and music may be added. The course of study extends over a period of five years, and the number of hours of recitation per week is limited to thirty, twelve of which are given to the study of Chinese classics. No tuition is to be charged in the schools established by the government.

Higher Primary School

The purpose of the higher primary school is to cultivate the moral nature of the young citizen, to enlarge his knowledge, and to strengthen his body. These schools are to be established in cities, towns, and villages. At least one such school is to be maintained by the government in each of these territorial divisions. Graduates of the lower primary school and children below the age of fifteen having equivalent preparation are admitted. The curriculum includes the following nine subjects of study: morals, Chinese classics, Chinese language, mathematics, history, geography, nature study, drawing, and physical culture. Courses in hand work, agriculture, and commerce may be added. The course extends over a period of four years, with thirty-six hours of recitations per week, twelve of which are given to Chinese classics. Higher primary schools established by the government are to charge for tuition, the amount to be determined by local conditions and the financial ability of the community.

Middle School

The middle school corresponds very closely to the American high school. Its aim is to provide higher general education for children between the ages of fifteen and nineteen, so as to prepare them to enter political and industrial life or the various higher institutions of learning. The middle school is to be limited to graduates of the higher primary school, but in case the number of graduates from the primary schools exceeds the number of vacancies in the middle school, an examination is to be given to eliminate the less desirable ones. A tuition fee is charged according to local conditions. The course of study is five years and includes the following twelve subjects: morals, Chinese classics, Chinese literature, foreign languages, history, geography, mathematics, biology, physics and chemistry, civics and economics, drawing, and physical culture. The number of recitations per week is thirty-six throughout the course. Chinese classics and literature continue to receive emphasis, occupying thirteen hours per week for the first two years, fourteen hours for the third, and twelve for the fourth and fifth.

Higher School or Provincial College

The higher school corresponds to the last years of the German gymnasium, or the French lycée, and to the first years of the American college. Its aim is to prepare students to take up work in the colleges of the university. Such a school is to be established in the capital city of each province and to be maintained by the province in which it is situated. Graduates of middle schools are to be admitted. Tuition is charged. The curriculum requires three years of thirty-six hours per week. It provides for three courses of study: Course A preparing students to enter the university colleges of Chinese classics, political science and law, literature, and commerce; Course B preparing for the colleges of science, agriculture, and engineering; Course C for the college of medicine. The curriculum lays great stress on modern languages, with the object of preparing students to read foreign books with ease.

University

Universities are to be established in Peking and in the provinces. Graduates of provincial colleges are admitted. Tuition is charged. The university is to have the following colleges: 1, Chinese classics; 2, law; 3, literature; 4, medicine; 5, science; 6, agriculture; 7, engineering; and 8, commerce. All the courses outlined for the colleges cover three years except the two parallel courses in the law college and the course for physicians in the college of medicine, which require four years' work. The college of Chinese classics has eleven courses each requiring four hours per week. The college of law has two courses, political science and law, each requiring twenty-four hours per week. The college in literature has nine courses, each requiring twenty-four hours. In the medical college two courses are outlined: the course for physicians, and the course in pharmacy. The college of science has six courses of study: mathematics, astronomy, physics, chemistry, zoölogy and botany, and geology. The college of agriculture has four courses: agriculture, agricultural chemistry, forestry, and veterinary medicine. The college of engineering has the following courses: architecture, mechanical engineering, naval architecture, technology of arms, electrical engineering, civil engineering, chemical engineering, technology of explosives, mining and metallurgy. The college of commerce has three courses: banking and insurance, trade and traffic, and taxes and customs. The number of hours for the different courses varies widely.

School of Research

This is to be a graduate school, admitting graduates of the university colleges and other applicants who can pass the examination for admission. The work covers a period of five years, two of which must be passed in residence. Satisfactory completion of a thesis, embodying the result of an investigation, is required of all students for graduation.

Normal Schools

Normal schools are of three kinds: the higher normal, the lower normal, and the industrial training school. The law requires that all expenses of a normal-school student be paid by the local authorities, unless the student prefers to be self-supporting.

Lower Normal School

The aim of the lower normal school is to train teachers for the lower and higher primary schools. Each prefecture is to maintain at least one such school capable of receiving one hundred and fifty students or more, and each provincial capital is to have one to accommodate three hundred students. Under special circumstances two or three prefectures are allowed to establish one school in common, in which case the capacity of the school must be three hundred instead of one hundred and fifty. The curriculum of the lower normal school consists of twelve subjects: ethics, Chinese classics, Chinese literature, education, history, geography, mathematics, nature study, physics and chemistry, penmanship, drawing, and physical culture. Two courses of study are outlined, a long course and a short course. The long course covers five years of forty-four weeks each, having thirty-six hours per week. The short course, consisting of one year's work of thirty-six hours a week, is offered to meet the immediate need of teachers.

Higher Normal School

The higher normal school is to train men to fill teaching and administrative positions in lower normal and middle schools. The plan was to establish in each provincial capital one higher normal school large enough to accommodate at least two hundred and forty-eight students. The curriculum provides for three kinds of courses, general, special, and graduate. The general course, taken by all students, requires one year of thirty-six hours a week, distributed among eight subjects: ethics, Chinese classics, Chinese literature, Japanese language, English language, logic, mathematics, and physical culture. There are four special courses of three years each, and requiring thirty-six hours per week. They are designed to prepare teachers of special subjects, as follows: Course A emphasizes Chinese literature and foreign languages; Course B emphasizes geography and history; Course C emphasizes mathematics, physics, and chemistry; and Course D emphasizes botany, zoölogy, bacteriology, and physiology. The following subjects are common to all four courses: ethics, classics, education, psychology, and physical culture. The graduate course offers ten subjects, of which the student must elect five. After completing his course of study, he is required to write a thesis. The course is one year in length, and the number of hours is left to the discretion of the faculty.

Industrial Teachers' Training School

The purpose of industrial teachers' training schools is to train teachers for industrial schools and for apprentice schools. They admit graduates of middle schools and lower normal schools. There are three kinds of industrial training schools, namely, the agricultural, the commercial, and the mechanical. They are usually established as subordinate departments in higher and middle schools, although they may be established independently, especially in provinces where industrial colleges and high schools are not yet in existence.

The curriculum for both agricultural and commercial departments extends through a period of two years, while the mechanical department offers a full course of three years and a short course of one year. The agricultural curriculum covers twenty-three subjects of study; the commercial, fifteen. Both the full and the short course of the mechanical department consist of six parallel çourses. Each of the parallel courses for three years' work covers from fourteen to nineteen subjects, and each parallel course for the one year's work covers from eight to eleven subjects. The subjects are either essential or supplementary to the particular subject which the student chooses for specialization.

Industrial Schools

The system of industrial schools consists of the following: apprentice school, primary industrial, industrial supplementary, middle industrial, and higher industrial. The higher industrial admits graduates of the middle schools, the middle industrial admits graduates of the higher primary, and the primary industrial admits graduates of the lower primary. The industrial supplementary school admits those students who have been in a higher primary school for two years and those already in industrial pursuits who wish to improve their knowledge. The apprentice school admits graduates of lower primary. In all cases an entrance examination is required of the students. Tuition is charged according to the financial ability of the local community in which the schools are established. The course of study of the primary industrial school varies from two to three years; the middle industrial school has a two-year preparatory and a three-year regular course; and the higher industrial has a preparatory course of one year and a regular course of three or four years. The course of study in the industrial supplementary school is three years, while the length of time required to finish the different courses in the apprentice school varies from six months to four years.

Special Schools

Two kinds of special schools are also provided, namely, I Hsüeh Kuan, the school of languages, and Chin Shih Kuan, or the school of doctors. The former is to train interpreters, and admits graduates of middle schools. The course is five years, of thirty-six hours per week. English, French, Russian, German, and Japanese are taught, and each student is required to specialize in one of these languages. The Chin Shih Kuan is to give the Chin Shih and the Hanlin, graduates of the old system of examinations, an opportunity to study western learning, believing that a general education is necessary to prepare them for their future official duties. The course is three years, having class-room work amounting to four hours per week. Eleven subjects of study are prescribed.

Abandonment of the Examination System

During these years of educational reform the question of how to improve the examination system has not escaped the attention of the Empress Dowager and her followers. In 1901 an edict was issued abolishing for the second time the use of the "eight-legged essay" in the examinations for literary degrees, and substituting in its place short and practical essays on current topics. It also abolished once more the military examination system. These reform measures, however radical they may have appeared at the time, were soon found to be insufficient; for it was discovered that as long as the examination system was in force little time was given to modern learning, and students would continue to follow the beaten track in their studies. Although modern education had been encouraged for some time, still few modern schools had been established, and men of means hesitated to make voluntary contributions toward their establishment. The leaders of reform now became convinced that in order to give the modern educational system a fair chance of development the old examination system must be entirely abolished. But to abolish without previous notice a system that had practically become the very bone and sinew of the Chinese body politic was too revolutionary a step for even the most radical of the leaders of reform. In 1903 a memerial was presented to the Throne by three of China's greatest statesmen, Chang Chih Tung, Chang Pai Hsi, and Jung Ching, in which was embodied an elaborate system for gradually abolishing the examination system. In this memorial they expressed the belief that if the modern system of schools as had been outlined were fostered and supervised by the viceroys and governors, the modern colleges would be able in ten years to furnish a sufficient number of young men capable of rendering efficient service to the country, but this result could not be secured unless it were made known that the examination system was to be abolished. However, ere long this gradual way of abolishing the system appeared to be too slow in the minds of those seriously interested in the progress of educational reform. In 1905 Yüan Shih Kai and others once more memorialized the Throne, declaring that the act of abolishing the examination system would not be violating ancient custom, but rather following it, for in early antiquity candidates for public office were all selected from public schools. The memorialists pointed out the fact that the wealth and power of Japan and of the countries of the west had their foundation in nothing else than their own schools, and that as China was just then passing through a crisis fraught with difficulties she was in immediate need of men of talent with a modern training. They asserted that unless these old-style examinations were abolished at once the people would hesitate to enter the modern schools, and that if China wished to see the spread of modern knowledge, she must first do away with the old way of studying for the examinations. This plea for the new education on the part of one of the most experienced statesmen was effective; for in 1905 an edict was issued abolishing at once the system of examinations which had its origin in the very dawn of history. With its disappearance the transition from the traditional education to modern education was practically complete.

CHAPTER V

THE CONSTRUCTION OF A MODERN EDUCATIONAL SYSTEM[1]

(1905–1911)

The short time extending between 1905 and the end of the Manchu dynasty (1911) constitutes the period during which the modern educational system outlined by the special Commission in 1903 was actually carried out. Readjustments had to be made in every direction, not only to the educational agencies of the system that had been abolished, but also to the political and social changes that were being rapidly introduced. At the same time the movement to introduce modern learning witnessed a rapid expansion and growth, the like of which China had never seen. Memorials, edicts, and regulations, relating to different phases of the new educational system, which appeared during these eventful years, fill no fewer than twelve volumes. To consider minutely the different problems dealt with would be out of proportion to the plan of this study, but it is necessary for us to trace the leading steps that were taken in the construction of the modern educational system in order to appreciate the work of reorganization now engaging the attention of the new republic.

The Ministry of Education

The first step in the up-building of the new system of education was taken in December, 1905, when the Throne, in response to a joint recommendation of the Department of the State (Cheng Wu Ch'u) and the Department of Education (Hsüeh Wu Ch'u) created a ministry of education charged with the duty of superintending and controlling the new educational system and of furthering the cause of the new education through-

---

[1] The data of this chapter are taken mainly from "Ta Ching Chiao Yu Fa Ling," or Educational Laws of the Manchu Dynasty.

out the Empire. The new ministry took precedence of the Ministry of Rites, which had been in charge of educational affairs. By the same decree the ancient national university, known as Kuo Tzŭ Chien in later dynasties, but as Cheng Chun in early antiquity, was amalgamated with the new ministry, and Jung Ching, the assistant grand secretary and chancellor of the Hanlin Academy, was appointed the first president of the new ministry. During the period under consideration, the Ministry of Education was one of the eleven great executive departments of the state: viz., the Ministry of Foreign Affairs, the Ministry of Civil Offices, the Ministry of Home Affairs, the Ministry of Finance and Paymaster General's Department, the Ministry of Rites, the Ministry of War, the Ministry of Judicature, the Ministry of Agriculture, Works, and Commerce, the Ministry of Dependencies, the Ministry of Education, and the Ministry of Communication.

According to the plan approved by the Throne in 1906, the Ministry of Education was organized as follows: It had at its head a president, two vice-presidents, two first-class assistants, two second-class assistants, and four third-class assistants. These officers were assisted by five departments into which the Ministry was divided, namely, the department of general supervision, the department of technical or special education, the department of publication, the department of industrial education, and the department of finance. Three of the five departments were sub-divided into three bureaus each, the others each consisting of two bureaus. Each department had a senior secretary in charge, and each bureau had a second-class secretary and one or two third-class secretaries. Provision was also made for the creation of a number of national inspectors, four kinds of advisers, a bureau for the preparation and publication of text-books, and a set of officers to take special charge of the duties formerly belonging to the National University (Kuo Tzŭ Chien) which had been amalgamated with the Ministry of Education. The Ministry of Education so constituted codified educational laws, appointed national inspectors (twelve in number), had the power to remove from office any educational officers found inefficient, nominated provincial commissioners of education, and, in short, had absolute control of all educational matters in the country, save those special phases of education which were under the immediate direction of minor and subsidiary central authorities.[2]

Aim of the Modern Educational System

Early in 1906, in response to a memorial of the Ministry of Education, a decree was issued in which the aim of the modern educational system was set forth as to develop in the minds of the young generation the following virtues: loyalty to the emperor, reverence for Confucius, devotion to public welfare, admiration for the martial spirit, and respect for industrial pursuits. The same decree declares that the first virtue is needed for the development of patriotism, the second to uphold morality, the third to foster a co-operative spirit, the fourth to make possible a strong nation capable of maintaining her own existence and freeing herself from foreign aggression, and the fifth to make possible the full utilization of China's natural resources for the benefit of the country as well as the life of the people. Here, as in the traditional system, the aim of education is to promote the welfare of the state as a collection of individuals in themselves unimportant, rather than to develop the individual into a dignified and integral member of the state as in the Old Greek education It is not within our province

[2] The subsidiary central authorities and their educational duties are as follows: The Metropolitan Board of Education has charge of all the normal, middle, and primary education in the capital. The Ministry of Foreign Affairs is in partial control of Tsing Hua College, the preparatory school established with the surplus of the indemnity fund returned by the government of the United States. The Ministry of War is in charge of the military schools scattered throughout the country and of the naval academies at Foochow, Tientsin, Chefoo, and Nanking. The Ministry of Rites continues to have charge of unfinished matters relating to successful candidates of the old examination system already abolished. It has also taken part in legislation relating to student uniforms, school holidays, and other matters that have to do with public ceremonies. The Ministry of Dependencies has some control over the education of the outlying provinces, such as Tibet, Mongolia, and Manchuria. Schools of telegraphy, for the training of employees for the telegraph administration, are under the charge of the Ministry of Communications. The Ministry of Agriculture, Works, and Commerce has supervision of a certain number of special industrial and apprentice schools in the country. The Ministry of Civil Offices has charge of the awarding of degrees and official appointments to graduates of higher schools. In 1908 imperial permission was given to the Ministry of Finance to establish a school of finance in Peking, which is still under the charge of this ministry. For a number of years the T'ung Wen Kuan (a school of languages) in Peking and the T'ung Wen Kuan in Canton were in the hands of the educational department of the Chinese Maritime Customs. The former was amalgamated with the Imperial University in 1902, but the latter survived until the period under consideration. In 1908 a school for the training of men to fill positions in the customs service was established in Peking by the Controller of Customs, and remains in his charge.

to raise here the oft-repeated question whether man exists for the state or the state for man. Shall the man educate himself that the state may endure, or shall the state educate man that he may prosper? Suffice it to say that these opposing aims of education, both represented in the history of education, are dependent upon opposite conceptions of the State.[3]

Official Regulations of 1906

From the standpoint of the educational historian who wishes to make a close study of China's attempt to make her own the educational experience and the newest methods of the modern world, the year 1906 will be considered as one of vital importance. For in this year several regulations drawn up by the new Ministry of Education, relating to the organization and administration of the educational system, were put into practice after receiving the sanction of the Throne. One of these official regulations had for its purpose the unification and regulation of the educational associations which were being rapidly developed throughout the country. Another set of regulations had to do with the detailed organization of the national system of educational administration, including the Ministry of Education and a system of national inspection. A third set of regulations dealt with the system of educational administration in the provinces and in smaller local areas, including the provincial boards of education, a system of provincial inspection, and the organization of local boards for the promotion of education. Through these regulations the new public educational system, outlined in the previous period, was developed to a high degree of theoretical completeness though it may have fallen short in practice.

National Educational Survey

A really statesmanlike step in the administration of education was taken in 1907, when the Ministry of Education instructed the provincial commissioners of education to require the local authorities of each prefecture, sub-prefecture, department, and district, to make a careful investigation of the conditions existing in their respective areas, and to report the result of their

[3] Cf. Perry: Outlines of School Administration, pp. 14-15.

findings for the purpose of obtaining some kind of basis or guide in the determination of future educational policy. The information called for in the investigation included the following topics: the characteristics of the physical environment; the census; the racial, intellectual, moral, and religious characteristics of the population; their customs, modes of life, and state of culture; their financial ability, including the total amount of taxes collected and the various forms of local taxes available; and the status of education, such as the number of pupils, the method of support, and the amount of funds available for educational purposes. The investigation thus called for and carried out amounted to no less than a national survey of the educational possibilities of the country and of the thousand and one factors which must be taken into consideration in the installation of a system of national and popular education.

Educational Programs to Prepare the People for Constitutional Government

Along with the development of modern education there has been going on a movement toward the adoption of a representative government. By an imperial decree of 1908 a constitutional form of government was promised and steps were taken to prepare for its adoption. The Ministry of Education, recognizing the fact that the success of a popular government is greatly dependent upon a high degree of intelligence and morality in the people, prepared a special educational program for the purpose of hastening the development of the new system of popular education. The program, setting forth the various steps to be taken by the Ministry as well as the provinces, covers a period of eight years beginning with 1909 and ending in 1916, the time appointed for the establishment of the constitutional form of government. The program is indeed an imposing one, and if it had been carried out there would have been developed in China by the end of 1916 an educational system comparing favorably with the most highly developed systems of the world. The program in question, though duly sanctioned by the Throne and immediately put into practice, had to be cast aside, for the Throne, in answer to frequent memorials, soon brought down the date of adopting the constitutional government from 1917 to 1913. This shortening of the period of preparation by four years necessitated the adoption of a shorter program than the one previously proposed. As a result, a new general program giving the steps of greatest importance and those of secondary importance was adopted at the close of 1910, and at the beginning of 1911 another program for the following two years was submitted by the Ministry of Education and sanctioned by the Throne. No one suspected then that even these programs would be cast aside by the political upheaval which resulted in the downfall of the Manchu dynasty.

System of National Inspection

The system of national inspection of education outlined in one of the official regulations of 1906 was not put into practice until a more detailed plan had been drawn up in connection with the program for the preparation of constitutional government. During the latter part of 1909, immediately after the adoption of the detailed plan, the first group of inspectors was sent out to the provinces of Honan, Kiangning, Kiangsu, Anhui, Kiangsi, Hupeh, and Chekiang, and in the following year the second group was sent out to other provinces. The memorials of the Ministry of Education reporting the completion of these inspections, though general in character, throw much light on the status of education during that period, inasmuch as they contain not only accounts of merits and shortcomings but also recommendations as to how improvements and readjustments ought to be made. Since this first system of inspection has been revised under the republic, no description of it will be given here except a few general statements which may help us to understand the system newly introduced.

The national inspection of education represents the field work of the Ministry of Education. According to the plan of 1909 the country was divided into twelve inspectorial divisions, each consisting of two or three provinces. Each division had two inspectors, appointed annually, but each year only four of the twelve divisions were inspected. Thus every three years completed one round, and each division had an inspection every third year. The plan provided that at least one of the two inspectors of every division must be a man thoroughly familiar with one or more modern languages and the various sciences, in order that he might be qualified to judge the work done in and above the middle school. The other qualifications required of inspectors were broadmindedness and familiarity with educational principles. The duties of the inspector were twofold; first, to keep the Ministry of Education well informed as to the progress of education in the provinces to which he is assigned, and second, to encourage and help the provinces in their attempt to carry out the various educational policies.

First Central Educational Conference, 1911

In 1911 the Ministry of Education, with the sanction of the Throne, brought into existence an auxiliary educational agency of great importance known as the Central Educational Council (Tsung Yang Chiao Yu Hui). This council is an adaptation of the Higher Educational Council of the Japanese educational system, and the duties of the council are similar to those of the Consultative Committee of the English Board of Education and those of its prototype, the Comité Consultatif in France. It is an advisory council and was called into existence for the purpose of obtaining the knowledge, the experience, and the results of the deliberation of the educators of the country with a view to promoting the cause of education and hastening its progress by helping the Ministry of Education to adopt a sound educational policy. The council was to be established in Peking and to hold its session of thirty days during the summer vacation. The discussions of the council while in session were to be confined to problems relating to schools of the rank of the middle school and those below it. The members of the council included representatives of the Ministry of Education, the Ministry of Home Affairs, the Ministry of Army and Navy, the Metropolitan Board of Education, provincial boards of education, provincial inspectors, provincial educational associations, retired national inspectors, heads of schools under the immediate supervision of the Ministry of Education, and heads of normal, middle, and elementary schools. The term of office was three years.

The first conference of the Central Educational Council was held in Peking in the summer of 1911. Over one hundred delegates from the provinces were present. Among the problems discussed were the following: compulsory education, cessation of the granting of official degrees to graduates of modern schools, training for military citizenship, government subsidy to primary education, supervision of lower normal schools by the provincial government, removing classics from the primary school and making hand work compulsory, unification of the mother-tongue, government subsidy to primary school teachers, and co-education in the lower primary school. Most of the measures recommended by the council were officially adopted by the Ministry, although the outbreak of the revolution in the fall of that year prevented their being put into operation.

Systems of Provincial and Local Administration of Education

The evolution of a system of provincial and local administration of education constitutes an important phase of the development of modern education in China. The system in existence prior to 1906 may be described in a few words. In each province there was an educational officer known as Literary Chancellor (T'i-tu-hsüeh-cheng); this office originated in the reign of Yung Cheng (1725-1735 A.D.), and was itself an adaptation of a similar office known as Superintendent of Learning (T'i-hsüeh-tao) created at the beginning of the Manchu dynasty in imitation of the practice of the Ming dynasty. This chancellor, through whom the Ministry of Rites came into contact with the provinces, exercised immediate control over the literary competitive examinations in the provinces. He was assisted by a director of studies located in each prefecture and a supervisor of studies in each district. In addition to these officials who had to do with the old educational system, there was found in most of the provinces a certain board of education known as Hsüeh Wu Ch'u, which had charge of all matters relating to the new educational movement.

In 1906, upon the recommendation of the Ministry of Education, a new administrative system was adopted to take the place of the one just described. The new scheme brought into existence as the head of the educational work of the province an officer known as Commissioner of Education (T'i-hsüeh-szŭ), who was appointed by the Throne upon the nomination of the Ministry of Education. In rank he occupied a position in the province similar to that occupied by the other two chief executive heads of the province, namely, the treasurer and the justice, and like them he was placed under the control of the viceroy or governor. The viceroy, in turn, was under the control of the Ministry of Education in matters relating to education. In ordinary matters, however, the Commissioner of Education was really the chief. In place of the old board of education (Hsüeh Wu Ch'u), a new board, known as Hsüeh Wu Kung So, was created. This board had six bureaus, each of which had one chairman and one vice-chairman at its head, who were appointed by the Commissioner of Education. The board also had one senior and five junior councillors whose duty was to assist the Commissioner in devising ways and means to carry out the educational program. The former was appointed by the Minister of Education with the approval of the Throne, and the latter by the Commissioner of Education himself. The system of 1906 also provided for each province six provincial inspectors whose duty it was to supervise and direct the educational work in the province. These inspectors were appointed by the viceroy or governor upon the nomination of the provincial commissioner.

In the smaller territorial divisions, such as prefectures, subprefectures, departments, districts, and villages, the local civil authorities were held responsible for carrying out the educational policy of the province,[4] their duties being supervisory and

[4] For the purpose of local government the provinces of China used to be divided into various administrative units, the chief of which are six, namely, fu, ting, chili ting, chou, chili chou, and hsien. A fu is a large portion or department of a province, under the general control of one civil officer immediately subordinate to the heads of the provincial government. A ting is a division of a province smaller than a fu and, like it, governed by an officer immediately subject to the heads of provincial government, or else forming a subordinate part of a fu. In the former case it is called chili, i.e., under the direct rule of the provincial government; in the latter case, it is called simply ting. A chou is similar to a ting, and like it either independent of any other division, or forming part of a fu. The difference between the two is that the government of a ting resembles that of a fu more nearly than that of a chou, that of the chou being simpler. The ting and chou of the class to which the term chili is attached may be denominated, in common with the fu, departments or prefectures; and the term chili may be rendered by the word independent. The subordinate ting and chou may both be called districts. A hsien, which is also a district, is a small division or subordinate part of a department, whether of a fu or of an independent chou or ting. These administrative divisions were made by the official regulations of 1906 into local units for the purpose of educational administration. Each of these larger areas was, however, subdivided into small areas known as hsüeh-ch'ü, or school districts, beginning with the regions within and near the walled city and extending toward the outlying districts, villages, and hamlets. Each school district contains about three to four thousand families. Sometimes one district includes two or three villages, and again more than ten villages are included in a single school district.

judicial in character. In each sub-prefecture, department, and district there was created a local bureau of education known as the Educational Exhorting Bureau (Ch'uan Hsüeh So) to take general charge of the educational work of the area. Each of these bureaus had one district inspector (Hsien Shih Hsüeh) who was its chief executive officer. He was appointed by the Commissioner of Education. For each school district there was also an officer responsible for the encouragement of education, known as the educational promoter (Ch'uan Hsüeh Yüan). He was appointed by the local authorities upon the recommendation of the director of the Educational Exhorting Bureau, who selected his candidates from among the local gentry deeply interested in education. This officer was a kind of field agent for the director of the bureau or for the bureau itself. Lowest in the scale of local authorities were the school trustees who were elected by the people to look after the interest of the school in the village or district, and to see that funds were provided for its maintenance.

Such in brief was the system of educational administration introduced in 1906 and in full operation between that year and 1911. At the beginning of the latter year a change was made in the local government through the introduction of a Council for Self-Government, known as Tzŭ Chih Chih, provided for in the program for the preparation of constitutional government. This change in the form of local government necessitated modifications in the educational administrative system. The educational work in the prefectures, departments, and districts, was now handed over to the Council for Self-Government, but in cities and villages it could be given to a new organization known as the Country School Union (Hsiang Hsüeh Lien Ho Hui). These unions were formed by groups of districts and villages which could not afford to support the necessary schools singly and they were therefore different from the schemes of consolidation found in the agricultural regions of the United States and Canada, where the desire to secure greater efficiency plays the leading part. These changes of administration were, however, introduced only in the more progressive districts where the Council for Self-Government had already been organized; elsewhere the system of 1906 continued in operation until the outbreak of the revolution, when further changes were made necessary.

Chinese Educational Missions Abroad[5]

The movement to send students abroad, started in a more or less haphazard way, soon developed so rapidly as to necessitate the creation of a system of control and of examination. Prior to 1907 Chinese students studying abroad were under the care of China's diplomatic representatives. In 1907 a special director was appointed to take charge of the students in Europe. In the following year an educational bureau was organized in the Chinese legation in Japan to take special charge of the students in that country. Since it was found difficult for one man to handle students scattered in different countries, similar bureaus were organized in 1909, in France, Germany, Russia, Belgium, and England,[6] each bureau being subject to the general supervision of the Chinese Minister. But two years later these bureaus were abolished and Chinese students in Europe are now under the direct control of the home government. In America the Chinese Minister was relieved in 1907 of the care of students by the Chinese Educational Mission, created to take special charge of the students sent out under the indemnity fund scholarships.[7] Beginning with 1913 all provincial students have also come under the care of this mission.

Examinations instituted for students sent abroad are of two kinds, those given to students before they leave China, for the purpose of finding out whether they possess the required qualifications, and those given after they return, in order to test their ability prior to giving them official appointments. The qualifications required of those who go abroad are graduation from the middle school or preparation equal to it, an understanding of the language of the country to which they are sent, and ability to enter special higher schools. In the summer of 1907 the Kiangsu Provincial Government held the first competitive examination for the selection of students to go abroad. This examination was unique in that it was the first one open

---

[5] Cf. King, H. E.: The Educational System of China as Recently Reconstructed, Chapter VIII.

[6] At first the director in charge of the educational bureau in Belgium also had charge of the students in England.

[7] Out of gratitude for the return to China by the United States of over $10,000,000 of the Boxer indemnity, China pledged herself to send to the United States 100 students each year for four years, and 50 students annually thereafter for twenty-eight years, in all 1,800 students.

to women. Out of six hundred students who made application, only seventy-two young men and ten young women were deemed qualified to enter the examination. After a three days' test, ten male and three female students were chosen, all of whom were qualified to do university work. In the following year a similar examination was held in Hangchow by the Chekiang Provincial Government. In 1909 the government selected by competitive examinations held in Peking the first group of students supported by indemnity fund to be sent to the United States. Out of about six hundred applicants, forty-seven students were chosen. Since then other examinations have been held by provincial and central governments, but in the case of those sent under the indemnity fund a preliminary course of training in the Tsing-Hua College is required. The first examination for returned students was held in Peking in 1905 under the direction of the Ministry of Rites. Degrees of Chin Shih, Hanlin, and Chü Jen were conferred upon successful candidates. Similar examinations were held each year by the Ministry of Education until 1911, when the system was abolished, along with the system of granting official degrees to college graduates.

Separation of the Civil Service Examination System from the Educational System

The abolishing of the system of granting official degrees by the government to graduates of colleges marks the separation of the civil service examination system from the educational system proper, and is of great significance in the history of education in China. In the course of our investigation we have observed that prior to the time of the T'ang dynasty all scholars chosen through competitive examinations became public officials. Beginning with the T'ang dynasty, the successful candidates of competitive examinations often failed to receive appointments, owing to the separation of the functions between the Board of Rites and the Board of Civil Offices. In spite of this fact, entrance to official life continued to be regarded as the goal of all higher intellectual training. When China first introduced the modern educational system, she followed the practice of the old examination system in conferring upon graduates of colleges official degrees, giving them the right to enter official life. But since the number of college graduates far exceeded the number of vacant public offices, many college graduates, though possessing official rank, necessarily failed to receive appointment in the government service. Aside from this state of affairs, which was in itself undesirable, this custom made the student class continue to look upon official life as the goal of education, while those who had no ambition to enter public service regarded as unnecessary all intellectual training beyond the mere rudimentary knowledge necessary for daily life and business. Indeed, so deeply imbedded in the constitution of the Chinese mind is this conception of education that even the abolishment of the system did not entirely succeed in removing it.

The immediate cause for abolishing the custom in question, however, was the introduction in that year of a new civil service system which made the examination of college graduates and the awarding of official titles unnecessary. Since it was realized, however, that doing away with degrees entirely would be disastrous to the modern educational system, a new system was adopted according to which graduation from the college in itself confers a degree, but such degree is merely academic in character and carries with it no privilege of official preferment. The various degrees provided for in the new system are as follows: graduates of a college or university receive the degree of Chin Shih; graduates of a higher school and other schools equal to it in rank receive Kung Shen; and graduates from a higher primary or a lower industrial school receive the degree of Sheng Yüan.

Changes and Developments in the School Organization

From the time of the adoption of the modern educational system (1903) to the close of the Manchu dynasty (1911), the changes in the school organization were along at least three lines: 1, in spreading modern education more widely; 2, in providing more diversified courses to meet the varying needs of pupils and communities; and 3, in cutting down the enormously overcharged program. These tendencies were quite in keeping with the spirit of the politics of the time, namely, the movement toward the adoption of a more popular form of government. At the same time the curricula of the various schools reveal the fact that the influence of the ancient classics still dominated the educational system. Evidently the transition from the old regime to the new had not yet been completed, at least not in the ideal of an educated man, which, like the ideal of a nation, requires a long period to change; for no sooner had the new system of education been adopted than there arose a loud outcry for the preservation of the ancient classics and their teachings. However, the dominance of the classics in the modern schools of China lasted for a very short time compared with the struggle against classics in the educational history of other nations. This fact will become clear later. Meanwhile we shall proceed to trace a few of the more important changes in the development of the following phases of the educational system: popular education, normal school education, industrial education, and higher and special education.

Popular Education

Lower primary school

According to the original plan of 1903, the course of study of the lower primary school was five years, and the number of recitations thirty per week. In 1909 the number of hours was increased to thirty-six per week owing to the addition of work in the Chinese language, but at the same time two shorter courses, one of four years and the other of three, were provided in order to meet the varying needs of local communities. In the following year, the four-year course having been found the most satisfactory one, the system of having three courses was replaced by a uniform course of four years. The number of hours was reduced to twenty-four per week for the first two years and thirty for the last two. In the revised curriculum Chinese classics and language continued to claim the largest portion of time, occupying fourteen hours per week during the first two years and fifteen during the last two.

Higher primary school

In 1910, owing to the change effected in the status of the lower primary school, the curriculum of the higher primary school was also revised and rearranged. Music was introduced as one of the optional studies. English was allowed in the third and fourth years of schools situated in treaty ports. With a view to unifying the mother-tongue, Mandarin was added to the curriculum as an additional study. The new course of study, however, remained four years in length with thirty-six hours of recitation per week.

Girls' primary schools

Prior to 1907 the importance of women's education had often been emphasized by governmental officials, and schools for girls had been established in the provinces, but no official action had been taken by the central government either to make provision for such schools or to regulate them. During that year imperial sanction was given to a set of regulations drawn up by the Ministry of Education which provided three forms of primary schools for girls similar to those for boys, namely: girls' lower primary school, girls' higher primary school, and girls' two-grade primary school, which last is a combination of the other two kinds of primary schools. The aim of girls' primary schools is similar to that of the boys' schools, namely, to promote the moral, intellectual, and physical development of the pupils. These girls' schools are established apart from those of boys. The lower primary school is for girls between the ages of seven and ten, and the higher for those of eleven to fourteen. The course of the lower primary school is four years, with a minimum of twenty-four hours per week and a maximum of twenty-eight. The higher primary school has a course of four years, and the time spent in recitations may vary from twenty-eight to thirty hours per week. The lower primary school has five required subjects of study, namely: morals, Chinese language, mathematics, sewing, and physical exercise. Music and drawing are optional subjects. In the first two years the Chinese language occupies twelve hours per week, and in the second two years, fourteen hours. In the higher primary school, in addition to the subjects found in the lower primary, the following are taught: history, geography, and science. The Chinese language occupies nine hours per week throughout the course. Sewing comes next in importance, with five hours per week in the first two years, and six in the last two years.

"Language-made-easy" school

In the educational program for the preparation of the constitutional government, drawn up in 1909, provision was made for the establishment of "language-made-easy" schools for the purpose of supplementing the work of the primary schools, whose number was not sufficient to meet the urgent demands of popular education. The lack of funds and teachers on the part of public authorities, and the want of money and time to go to school on the part of parents and children, were the factors which prompted the adoption of such a form of school. They are intended for children of very poor families who could not otherwise go to school at all, and also for illiterate adults. In these schools tuition is free, and books and supplies are also given free of charge. The session is from one to three hours a day, and is offered in the morning, in the afternoon, and in the evening. Graduates of the three years' course are admitted into the fourth year of the regular primary school. In 1911 a uniform course of two years, with twelve hours per week, was adopted. Graduates of the course are admitted to the third-year class of the regular primary school.

Half-day school

The establishment of half-day schools was sanctioned as early as 1906 upon the request of Liu Hsüeh Chien, a certain governmental official. The motives which called forth such schools, as well as their aims, are similar to those of the "language-made-easy" schools.

Reformed private schools

The educational authorities, realizing that the financial condition of the country would not permit for some time to come the provision of a sufficient number of modern schools for the masses, decided in 1910 to make use of the traditional schools that were found in great numbers throughout the country, such as schools maintained by the public funds for the education of the poor (I Hsüeh), schools established in the ancestral temples or other public buildings for the education of the children of the clan (Shu Shu), schools found in homes of the pupils, and those opened by teachers in their own homes. The plan was to reform these schools through the introduction of modern text-books and other measures. To carry out this purpose, special courses of study were drawn up for such schools, and graduates of schools which had adopted these courses of study were allowed to enter the schools of the regular system. An experiment was made in Peking in 1907 to test the practicability of the scheme. It was found that the private schools that were able to comply with the requirements numbered only twelve with an enrollment of over three hundred, whereas those not yet reformed were much more numerous. A scheme of inspectors and of reward was adopted to encourage their improvement. The result was surprising. During the first term of 1908 schools coming up to the standard numbered forty-two, with an attendance of over one thousand, and in the second term of the same year the number of these schools increased to eighty-nine, with over twenty-two hundred pupils. By the beginning of 1910 there were as many as one hundred and seventy-two such schools, with an enrollment of more than forty-three hundred pupils. The sum spent in awards amounted to only one thousand three hundred and seventy taels, but the result was one hundred and seventy-two good schools with four thousand three hundred pupils. News of the experiment spread throughout the country, and Peking's example was followed by the provinces, but the statistical result has not yet been made known owing to the outbreak of the revolution.

Middle school

In 1909, in response to the memorial of the Ministry of Education, imperial sanction was given to the provision of two parallel courses of study in the middle school, in order to meet the varying needs of the pupils. One of the courses was industrial, and the other literary, the former emphasizing science and the latter classics. The number of hours remained, as before, thirty-six per week throughout the course. In the beginning of 1911, the two courses of study were made lower in standard and more general in character. This change was due partly to the difficulty of securing qualified teachers and students, and partly to the expense of providing the necessary equipment. Moreover, there was also the desire to make secondary education less specialized, in the belief that the time had not yet come for China to provide such highly specialized courses in her secondary schools as are found, for instance, in Germany.

Normal School Education

Lower and higher normal schools

In 1906, under the instruction of the Ministry of Education, the following courses were added to the normal school curriculum: a one-year course in the lower normal school for the training of teachers of primary schools; a two-year selective course in the higher normal school to prepare teachers for prefectural normal and middle schools; and a five months' special course in physical culture for the training of teachers of this subject in primary schools. The options in the selective course were: (1) history and geography; (2) physics; (3) nature study; and (4) mathematics. Beginning with 1910, the selective course was abolished owing to the desire to improve the standard of teaching, but a course of two years was established for the purpose of preparing students to enter the general course of the higher normal school. In the lower normal school the curriculum was enriched by the addition of practice teaching in a one-room school and in a part-time school.

Girls' normal schools

The year 1907 will ever be memorable in the development of education for women, for in that year official provision was made for the creation not only of primary schools for girls but also of normal schools. The aim of these girls' normal schools was to train teachers for girls' primary schools. The plan was to establish eventually one government normal school in every department and district, but for the time being one in each prefecture and provincial capital was opened. Like the normal school for men, no tuition was charged. Graduates of girls' higher primary schools and those who had been in higher primary school for two years were admitted. The latter must, however, first enter the preparatory course for one year before taking the regular course. The curriculum consisted of four years of forty-five weeks each, with thirty-four hours of class work per week. The subjects taught were as follows: ethics, education, Chinese language, geography, history, mathematics, music, and physical culture. Where circumstances demanded, a preparatory course was added to the regular normal course, the subjects studied there being similar to those of the last two years of the girls' higher primary schools.

Industrial Education

In 1910, owing to the scarcity of schools giving industrial education, the alleged reason being that there were not enough industrial teachers in the country, a new system was adopted which provided for the establishment of industrial teachers' training schools of an elementary type, corresponding to the standard of the lower normal schools. Such institutions were to be established in both the higher and the lower industrial schools in the form of short courses. In the following year, finding that the number of teachers' training departments in industrial schools was very small, owing to financial difficulties, the Ministry of Education took further action, permitting industrial schools to offer a normal course consisting of the regular industrial course with the addition of principles and methods of teaching, educational law, etc. This move was made purely upon economic grounds, and was not intended to be continued indefinitely.

Higher and Special Education

In the field of higher and special education, changes and new developments also took place. The university preparatory school established in 1901 was abolished and its place taken by the higher school which is the regular preparatory school of the university. Many special schools came into existence and regulations for their control were drawn up. Among such special schools are the following: school of political science and law, school of medicine, school for the study of Manchu and Mongol languages, school for the preservation of ancient culture and literature, and Tsing Hua College for the preparation of students to be sent to the United States.

Control of Text-Books

In the development of the public educational system in China the importance of legislation directing the selection and designating the quality of text-books has not been overlooked. Prior to the creation of the Ministry of Education, the preparation of text-books was left to private initiative. Publishing houses wishing to insure their sales sent their books at times to the educational authority (Hsüeh Wu Ta Chen) in Peking for certification, but they were not required to do so. In the official regulations of 1906, provision was made for the creation of a special bureau in the Ministry of Education, charged with the responsibility of publishing text-books for the school system. By 1908 a series of readers for teaching Chinese characters in an easy way was completed. In the same year a series of citizens' readers made its appearance. These were soon followed by text-books for primary schools and manuals for primary school teachers. All the books published by the textbook bureau of the Ministry were distributed throughout the provinces and arrangements were made with provincial authorities to have them reprinted and used in public schools. At the same time the Ministry of Education adopted a system by which text-books published by individuals and publishing houses were certified and their use in schools authorized. Thus in the course of a few years a large number of text-books for the use of primary, middle, and lower normal schools were accepted by the Ministry. Text-books not certified by the Ministry were, however, not condemned and prohibited unless they were found to embody material contrary to the principles of the established government.

Status of Education at the Close of the Manchu Dynasty

In describing China's early attempts to introduce modern education a certain writer compared her to an inexperienced seabather in the act of taking his first plunge, touching the water and then running away, wading out and then tearing back; he does not dare to succumb to the allurements of the fascinating element, and though the sight of experienced bathers frolicking and playing hide and seek with the waves shoots an arrow of envy through him, he himself never makes the attempt. This comparison, no matter how true it was at the beginning, was certainly not true toward the close of the Manchu dynasty. At that time China's attitude toward modern education was far from the attitude of the timid sea-bather. She had taken not only her first plunge, but also the second, and even the third, and had fully determined to make modern education accessible to her people at any cost.

According to the third annual report of the Ministry of Education, published in 1911, there were in China during the year 1910, 52,650 modern schools of different types, including normal, industrial, and technical schools, with a student body numbering 1,625,534, a teaching force numbering 89,766, and a corps of administrative officers numbering 95,800. Aside from the schools there also existed during that year 69 boards of education, 722 local, provincial, and national educational associations, 1,558 educational exhorting bureaus, and 3,867 public lecture halls. The total income for educational purposes during that year was taels 25,331,171, and the expenditure for the same year was taels 24,444,309. The educational property possessed by the government was valued at taels 70,367,882. To these figures must be added those relating to Chinese students studying abroad.[8] In 1909 there were in Tokio 1,992 Chinese government students in the collegiate schools, and 395 in the military schools, making a total of 2,387 in that city alone. In addition there were also at least 2,500 private students. It is estimated that in 1910 there were not fewer than 5,000 private Chinese students in Japan, 150 of whom were women. In the same year there were in the United Kingdom some 140 Chinese government scholarship students and about an equal number of students supported by private funds. In Belgium there were about 70 government students; in France, 80; in Germany, 60; in Austria, 10; and in Russia, about 15. No statistics are available regarding the private students in these countries, as they were not under the direction of the Commissioner. In the United States the number of Chinese students in 1910 was estimated to be no fewer than 600.[9] The four provinces sending the largest number of students at that time were Kuangtung, Kiangsu, Chekiang, and Chili.

The record of modern education represented by these figures was made in the course of a few years. The following table prepared from data gathered from reports of the Ministry of Education gives some idea of the rate of increase in the number of different types of schools:

8 King, H. E.: The Educational System of China as Recently Reconstructed, p. 96.

9 *Chinese Students' Monthly*: March, 1910.

INCREASE IN NUMBER OF SCHOOLS

Year	*Governmental*	*Public*	*Private*	*Totals*
1905	3,605	393	224	4,222
1906	2,770	4,829	678	8,477
1907	5,224	12,310	2,296	19,830
1908	11,546	20,321	4,046	35,913
1909	12,888	25,688	4,512	43,086
1910	14,301	32,254	5,793	52,348

It is to be noticed that during the interval between 1905 and 1910 the number of governmental schools increased from 3,605 to 14,301, that of public schools from 393 to 32,254, and that of private schools from 224 to 5,793, making the average annual increase in each case remarkably high.[10] The number of students in all the types of schools has gained in an equally rapid manner. In 1903 there were only 1,274 students in the modern schools in China. Since then this small body has been steadily growing in size until we had in 1910 a school population of 1,625,534. The following table shows clearly the rapidity with which the number of students has increased during the eight years.

INCREASE IN NUMBER OF STUDENTS

Year	*Number of Students*
1903	1,274
1904	31,378
1905	102,767
1906	200,401
1907	547,064
1908	921,020
1909	1,301,168
1910	1,625,534

The statistics contained in the reports of the Ministry of Education show that different provinces were not in the same stage of development in the matter of offering educational opportunity to their people. Some have made rapid progress, while others are far behind. For example, in 1910 there were sixty-five educational associations in each of the two provinces of Chili and Szechuan, four in Kansu and only one in Heilungkiang. In the same year Chili and Szechuan had 152 and 145 educational exhorting bureaus respectively, while

[10] Government schools are supported by funds appropriated by the government treasury; public schools are those maintained by local public funds; and private schools are those established by individuals and maintained by donations.

Heilungkiang and Kirin had only 17 and 18 respectively. The same marked difference is found in the number of lecture halls. In that year Kweichow had 1,167 lecture halls; Szechuan, which leads in other educational matters, had 392; and Heilungkiang, which is the most backward province, had only 6. The same great divergence is shown in the number of students and schools. Among the factors which made this wide difference possible, are the following: (1) the relative financial strength of the province; (2) the size of the population; (3) the degree of intelligence of the population; (4) the external pressure, such as the influence of foreigners, etc.; (5) environment, such as geographical location; (6) the amount of effort put forth by the governmental officials and the people.

Some idea as to the quality of the work done in the schools of that period may be gained from the educational exhibits that were made in different parts of the country. At the Nanking Industrial Exhibition, held in 1910, more than 34,000 articles, including apparatus, text-books, charts, drawings, specimens of handwriting, etc., all products of the schools, were collected and exhibited, and the list of prizes awarded at the exhibition shows that no fewer than 900 prizes, which is about half of the total number of prizes given out, were awarded to articles in the educational exhibit. Much highly favorable comment was received from educators of the West who visited the exhibit. A similar but smaller collection of educational articles was sent to the exhibition held in Italy, and there again many prizes were received owing to the high standard reached both in skill and in content.

The status of education before the revolution is perhaps best seen by the influence which modern education had exerted upon the intellectual or thought life of the people. It is the opinion of many who are in a position to judge, that the schools and colleges of China contributed a great share to the revolutionary movement. Education evidently had created in the minds of the students, both young and old, an intense dissatisfaction with things as they were, and an earnest desire to better the condition of their country both socially and politically. Indeed, it has been repeatedly declared by Sun Yat Sen and others prominent in the revolutionary cause that education was the chief factor in the successful overthrow of the Monarchy and the establishment of the New Republic.

CHAPTER VI

REORGANIZATION OF EDUCATION UNDER THE REPUBLIC

Revolution of 1911 and its Effect Upon Education

The political revolution which broke out in Wuchang on October 10, 1911, resulting in the overthrow of the Manchu dynasty and the establishment of the republican form of government, turned the whole attention of the Chinese people for a time to their struggle for liberty, and temporarily checked the onward progress of modern education throughout the country. This setback was but a natural consequence of civil war, examples of which may be easily found not only in the history of China, but also in that of other nations. During the days of storm and stress, the funds intended for the maintenance of educational institutions had to be used for the support of the armies. Many of the school buildings were used as soldiers' quarters, and in not a few cases the entire school plant was destroyed by mobs, the books and apparatus being looted and scattered. In consequence, the activities of a large number of schools and colleges was either suspended or seriously crippled, especially those situated near the centers of disturbance, such as Chentu, Hankow, Wuchang, Nanking, and Canton. Many students whose sympathy was with the revolutionary movement volunteered for service in the field, either forming themselves into separate regiments or joining the regular army, some of them becoming influential leaders of the revolution. An equally large number of students organized associations for securing contributions of money toward the war fund. Still others volunteered to give lectures in public to supply the people at large with the facts of the revolution and to instruct them in the principles of the republic that was being advocated by the revolutionists. Thus during the days of revolution the cause of education received a blow from which it will require some time to recover.

Temporary Educational Policy of the Provisional Government

Soon after the Ministry of Education of the provisional government was organized in Nanking (January 9, 1912), it issued a dispatch[1] to the 17 republican tutuhs or governors of the various provinces embodying a policy governing popular education accompanied by a curriculum for middle school, primary school, and normal school. The said policy and curriculum were intended for temporary guidance and were eventually to be replaced by a complete new system drawn up after due consultation with the educators of the country. The dispatch urged the importance of promptly opening the schools which had been closed on account of the revolution, especially the primary schools. It demanded the use of only those text-books whose contents were in harmony with the spirit of republicanism, condemning the use of texts as well as works of reference published under the Manchu dynasty and containing sentiments and ideas inconsistent with the republican spirit, unless the objectionable parts had been entirely eliminated. In addition, it abolished the practice of awarding official degrees to graduates of primary and middle schools, shortened the course of study of both the middle school and the lower normal school from five to four years, and required the middle school to offer only one course in general culture instead of a literary and a technical course. The same dispatch also called upon the school authorities to put added emphasis upon manual work in primary schools and upon military drill as a form of physical exercise in schools above the higher primary, and to add the use of the abacus to the teaching of arithmetic in and above the third year of all lower primary schools. The most important and significant measures urged were, first, to permit boys and girls to attend the same lower primary school, and, second, to eliminate the classics entirely from the curriculum of primary schools. Both of these measures represented radical departures from the system in effect previous to the revolution, and were initiated to meet new conditions created by the political disturbances.

The temporary educational policy laid great emphasis upon the importance of social education, i.e., the diffusion of knowl-

---

1 *The Chinese Educational Review:* Vol. III, No. IV, Jan. 1912.

edge through quasi-educational institutions, such as public lectures, newspapers, libraries, and moving pictures. This movement was, no doubt, prompted by the belief that the stability of a republic depends largely upon the intelligence of its citizens, and by a realization of the facts that there still were manifold difficulties in the way of making a formal education accessible to all and that these quasi-educational institutions could be made to exert a strong educational influence upon the uneducated men and women, as well as upon those young people who were unable to go to school. Prompted by such convictions, the Ministry of Education sent a telegraphic message to the governors of the various provinces which had joined the republic, urging the importance of introducing, as a form of education, public lectures and also moving pictures of the profitable kind. They were asked to draw up provisional standards of procedure, to select and compile material to be embodied in the lectures, and to put the scheme into practice through local officials and enthusiasts for the cause. In addition, the dispatch urged that public funds should be appropriated for the purpose if necessary. Among the topics suggested for lectures were the following: the achievements of the revolution; the duties and privileges of republican citizenship; the importance of developing a military spirit; the importance of promoting the economic and industrial welfare of the country; and especially the importance of emphasizing public virtue. That the movement initiated by the Ministry of Education at this period exerted a great influence is shown by the response which it received from the provincial authorities as well as the people. The details of these activities, however, have no place in this general treatment. Suffice it to say that the Ministry of Education later created a special bureau known as the bureau of social education, the duty of which was to advance this whole movement of making education widespread through quasi-educational institutions.

Upon the election of Yüan Shih Kai as President of China (April 1, 1912), a new Ministry of Education was hastily formed, which instead of remaining in Nanking and representing only a portion of China, now made its headquarters in Peking in buildings formerly occupied by the Ministry of Education of the Manchu dynasty and represented the whole country, including its dependencies. Most of the activities of this Ministry during the early part of its existence were naturally of a preliminary character. For example, it called for a thorough investigation of all changes in educational matters that had taken place since the outbreak of the revolution.[2] It demanded the return to the proper authority of all properties that had been temporarily yielded up for military and other purposes during the revolution and subsequent to it. It required those who publish text-books for use below middle schools to submit sample copies to the Ministry for decision as to their suitability. It made new efforts to further the social educational movement started by the preceding administration and urged provincial authorities to organize a similar movement in the provinces, describing the steps that had been taken by the Ministry itself and by the Metropolitan Board of Education at Peking. There was, however, at least one measure taken during the early part of this period which was of great significance, and which merits special attention, namely, the calling of the Emergency Central Educational Conference.

Emergency Central Educational Conference, 1912

The conference which met in Peking (July 10th to August 10th) was called into existence for a purpose similar to that which prompted the calling of the first central educational conference in 1911, viz., to profit by the knowledge and experience of the educators of the country with a view to promoting the cause of education and hastening its progress by helping the government to adopt a sound educational policy. In order to insure the best results from the conference, every effort was made to secure fully qualified men, including graduates of normal schools in China or abroad who had had at least three years of experience in teaching, as well as educators of national renown. The membership of the conference was distributed as follows: two from each of the twenty-two provinces, including Mongolia and Tibet; one representing Chinese residing abroad; fifteen from the teachers and administrative officers of schools under the direct control of the Ministry of Education; ten from the Ministries of the Interior, of Finance, of Agriculture, Com-

---

[2] This and other activities of the Ministry mentioned in this paragraph were all reported by the current issues of the *Chinese Educational Review*.

merce, and Industry, of Army and Navy; and others specially invited by the Ministry of Education. The conference was conducted under the direction of the Minister. Among the problems presented for discussion were the following: school government; division between central control and local control of schools; education of Mongols, Mohammedans, and Tibetans; the giving of special privileges to elementary school teachers and the certification of these teachers; the worshipping of Confucius; the adoption of a national anthem; and the organization of a higher educational conference. In all, ninety-two problems were submitted to the conference for solution, but during the nineteen regular meetings that were held, only twenty-three of the more important of these were satisfactorily settled and action upon them recommended to the Ministry of Education. Although the body of educators forming the conference was invested with no legislative power, the suggestions and recommendations made after careful deliberation exerted a strong influence upon the educational policy of the country, as can easily be seen by comparing the resolutions of the conference with the measures taken later by the Ministry for the reorganization of the educational system.

New Aim of Education

The next step of importance taken by the Ministry was the promulgation of the aim of education, which shows a slight change from the one published early in 1906. That was to inculcate in those who go to school the following virtues: loyalty to the emperor, reverence for Confucius, devotion to public welfare, admiration for the martial spirit, and respect for that which is practical. Education is now conceived as a means of cultivating virtuous or moral character in the young.[3] This moral training is to be supplemented by an industrial and military education and rounded out by an aesthetic education. The chief emphasis, then, is placed on the cultivation of a moral or virtuous character (tao teh). This is in keeping with the old Confucian ideal, but just what is meant by "tao teh" is left for each one to interpret for himself. It is sufficiently clear, however, that it refers to public morality or virtues, for the

[3] See Educational Ordinance No. 2, September 2, 1912.

chief interest in providing such an education is said to be the welfare of the state,[4] so long as education does not impede the progress of the world or interfere with the development of the individual. Tsai Yüan Pei, the first Minister of Education, defined this ethical education as that education which instills into the minds of the people the right knowledge of Liberty, Equality, and Fraternity.[5] The conception of education here given is voiced in the three personal messages of the Minister of Education issued at this period to the educational administrators, teachers, and students of the country.[6]

Reorganization of the Administrative System

The first step in the reorganization of the educational system was taken when President Yüan Shih Kai issued the first educational ordinance[7] announcing the scheme for reorganizing the Ministry of Education which had been passed by the National Assembly. According to this new scheme, the Ministry has at its head the Minister of Education, who has general charge of all matters relating to education and general supervision of all the schools of the country together with all public buildings under the immediate control of the Ministry. The Minister is assisted by many officers. Aside from those offices which are common to all ministries, there are provided sixteen inspectors and ten experts in art and science. The inspectors are appointed by the President of the Republic on nomination of the Minister, and the experts are appointed by the Minister himself. The work of the Ministry is carried on by one general council and three bureaus, instead of five bureaus as was the case before the revolution. The general council has special charge of all matters relating to schools under the direct control of the Ministry, teachers in public schools, educational associations, investigations and compilations, school hygiene, organization and maintenance of school libraries, school museums, and educational exhibits. The three bureaus are as follows: 1, bureau of general education; 2, bureau of technical or profes-

---

4 Consult Proceedings of the Central Educational Conference.

5 China Mission Year Book, 1913, p. 254.

6 For the full text of the messages consult *Chinese Educational Review*, September, 1912.

7 Educational Ordinance No. 1.

sional education; and 3, bureau of social education. The bureau of general education is in charge of all matters relating to normal schools, middle schools, primary schools, kindergartens, and schools for all forms of defectives, including the deaf and the blind. It also has charge of matters relating to school attendance and the selection and certification of teachers. The bureau of technical or professional education has charge of all affairs relating to universities and colleges, higher technical schools, the sending of students abroad, the national observatory and the preparation of the governmental almanac, the society of doctors of philosophy, the association for the unification of the mother tongue, the association of examiners of medical doctors and pharmacists. In addition, this bureau has control of all matters relating to societies of arts and sciences, and to the conferring of degrees. The bureau of social education is in charge of all affairs relating to the regulation of public ceremonies, to museums and exhibits, music, literature, and the stage, the investigation and collection of relics, popular education and public lecture bureaus, public and circulating libraries, and last of all, the compilation, the investigation, and the planning of popular education.

In 1913 a new scheme of national inspection of education was adopted to replace the one introduced in 1906. This plan divides the country into eight inspectorial divisions instead of twelve as under the old system. The new divisions are as follows: 1, Chili, Fengtien, Kirin, and Heilungkiang; 2, Shantung, Shansi, and Honan; 3, Kiangsu, Anhui, and Chekiang; 4, Hupeh, Hunan, and Kiangsi; 5, Shensi and Szechuan; 6, Kansu and Hsinkiang; 7, Fukien, Kuangtung, and Kuangsi; 8, Yunuan and Kweichow. Mongolia and Tibet are temporarily made special territorial divisions of inspection coming under special regulations. Each territorial division is provided with two inspectors of general and social education, who may secure assistance from the Ministry of Education. The regular period of inspection extends from August 20 to June 10 of the following year, but special inspections may be conducted at any time under special order from the Ministry of Education. The territory to be inspected every year is to be determined by the Ministry of Education on every occasion. Civil officials possessing one of the following qualifications may be employed as inspectors: (1) graduation from a Chinese or foreign university or from a higher normal school, with one or more years' experience in educational work; (2) three or more years of experience as the head or instructor of a normal or middle school; (3) three or more years' experience as an educational administrator. The things which the inspector is expected to look into are as follows: educational administration, educational conditions in schools, school finance, school hygiene, conditions relating to the work of educational officers, social education and its agencies, and matters especially indicated by the Minister of Education. The inspector may, however, also express his opinion to the local educational authorities regarding the following matters, violation of educational laws, matters decided upon by the Ministry of Education, school instruction and management, social education and agencies promoting it, as well as special matters suggested by the Minister of Education. The office of inspector is thus shorn of all the arbitrary powers it possessed under the old system, the duties left to the office being merely advisory in character. This change is indicative of the fact that under the new government the central authority has become less arbitrary, while local authorities have assumed more power of self government.

The system of provincial and local administration of education, like the political administrative system now in force, is as yet provisional in character, and is subject to radical changes. The practice in vogue in the various provinces is moreover far from being uniform. In most of the provinces there is a department of education in place of the former bureau of education. This department of education differs from the bureau of education in that the former is an integral part of the provincial administration, while the latter was an organ independent of the provincial administration. At the head of the department there is either the chief of the department or the commissioner of education, who is appointed by the president of the republic and is responsible to him. The department has also a number of provincial inspectors appointed by the governor of the province. In the districts[8] the local board of education, known as Ch'uan Hsüeh So, has been abolished and its duties

[8] Since the establishment of the republic the territorial division known as "fu" has been abolished.

have been transferred to the bureau of education (Hsüeh Wu K'u). The latter differs from the former in the same way as the present provincial department of education differs from the former provincial bureau of education, namely, while the former is an authority distinct from the local administration, the latter was an integral part of the district administration. The new bureau has a chief appointed by the magistrate of the district (Ming Cheng Chang) and a district inspector appointed by the same authority. In cities, towns, and villages, educational affairs are in the hands of certain of the local gentry (Tung Shih) who are selected by the people to look after the welfare of the local community. This body of men employs a special educational officer (Hsüeh Wu Chuan Yuan) to carry on the educational work of the community.

Reorganization of the School System

The chart on page 119 embodies the system of schools that has been introduced since the establishment of the republic.

The period of four years in the lower primary school is to be one of compulsory education. After completing the course therein, the pupils may enter a higher primary school or an industrial school. When a pupil has completed the three-year course in a higher primary school, he may enter a middle school, a normal school, or an industrial school of the A class. Supplementary courses offering continuation work are provided for those graduates of both the lower and the higher primary schools who for one reason or another cannot go to the school of a higher grade. Two years are required to complete these courses. After graduation from a middle school, a pupil is qualified to enter the preparatory department of a university, of a professional school, or of a higher normal school. The preparatory department of a university covers a period of three years, and the collegiate department three or four years according to the subject selected. The normal school requires one year's preparatory work, and itself has a four-year course, while the higher normal school course covers three years, following a year of preparatory work. Industrial schools are of two kinds, A and B, each having a three-year course. The professional school requires one year's preparatory work, and has a three or four-year course according to the subject. The age-scale

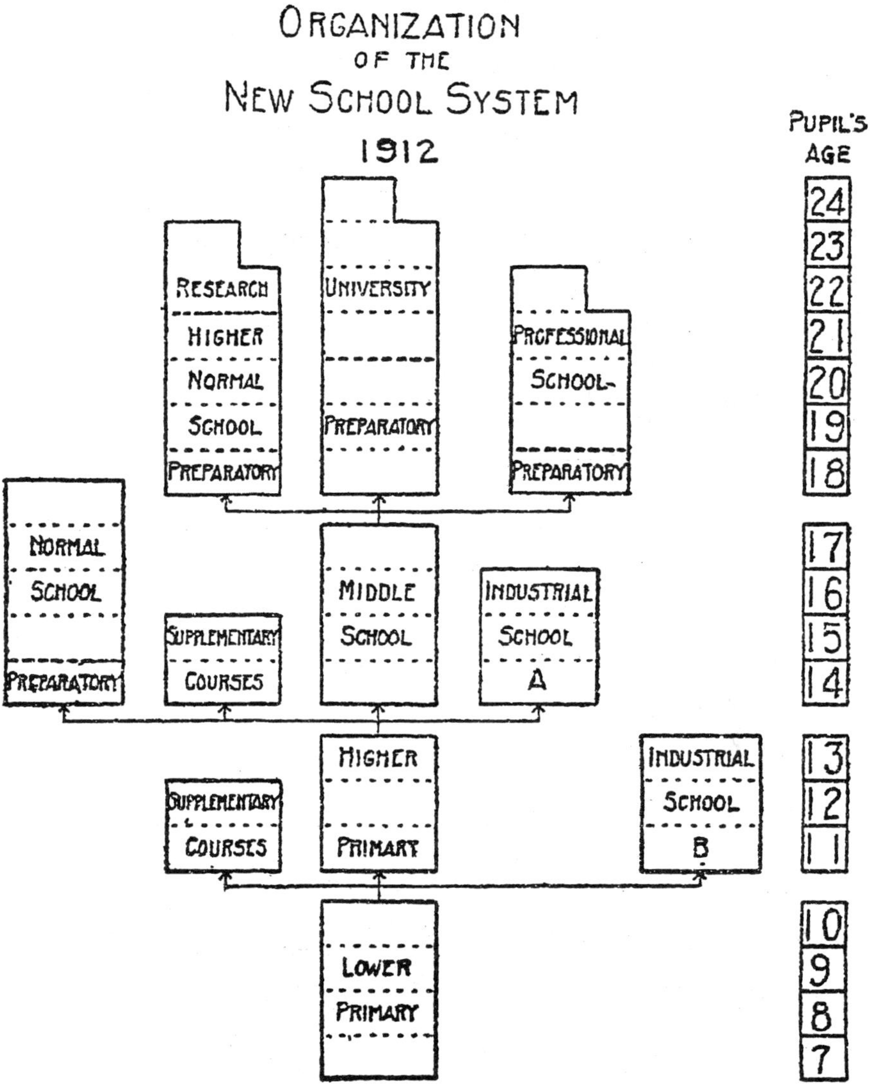

N. B. The higher normal school may also offer an elective course and one providing for specialization, each lasting two or three years.

to the right of the chart serves merely as a standard, and should not be taken as fixed. The time occupied by the course of studies may be extended or shortened according to the nature and locality of the school. This organization of the new system of schools differs from the one which existed before the revolution in the following respects: the course of study of the higher primary school is shortened from four years to three, that of the middle school from five to four; the higher school is changed into college preparatory, and the period of five years formerly set for post-graduate work in the university has been made indefinite. Thus the length of the period required to climb the entire educational ladder is shortened by several years. This change must be regarded as an improvement over the former system, inasmuch as it makes it possible for a larger number of children to graduate from the higher primary and middle schools.

With this general scheme in mind, we are now ready to examine in a more detailed way the organization of the new school system as well as the new curriculum introduced since the establishment of the republic.

Primary Schools

The aims of primary education are as follows: (1) to secure the physical and mental development of the child; (2) to lay the foundation of the virtues of citizenship; and (3) to develop in children the knowledge and ability necessary for them to make their way in the world. The primary schools as before are of two kinds, the lower primary school and the higher primary school, although the two may be combined.

Whereas before the revolution the responsibility of establishing primary schools was not placed upon any specific authority, the new republic definitely assigns this duty to cities, towns, and villages. Two or more villages may unite to establish schools by forming a school union, in case their financial resources do not enable them to support schools singly. Such school unions may create territorial divisions for the establishment of primary schools, and also special officers to manage their educational affairs. Under special conditions, district officials may designate certain schools established by private individuals to take the place of city, town, or village schools. Higher primary schools are established by districts. The number and the location of higher primary schools are to be planned and determined by district officials after due consultation with the district assembly. After having established a sufficient number of lower primary schools to accommodate all the children of school age in their respective jurisdictions, cities, towns, and villages may also establish higher primary schools either singly or conjointly, if they have financial resources beyond the amount needed for the maintenance of lower primary schools, but before so doing they must secure permission from the chief administrative officials of the district. The establishment, organization, or abolition of any primary school must first receive the sanction of the chief of the district officials. In case of higher primary schools, the district administrative official should make due report to the governor of the province. Kindergartens, schools for the blind and dumb, and other schools corresponding to primary schools are dealt with in the same way as the primary school.

The gentry of the city, town, or village, and the president of the school union, under the direction of the chief of the district administrative officials, control all the primary schools within their respective jurisdictions. Higher primary schools established by the revenue of the district are controlled by the chief district administrative official. He may cause the chief administrative official of the city, town, or village to render assistance to the educational work of his territory, under the direction of the gentry of the city, town, or village, or the president of the school union. All educational affairs entrusted to the head and teachers of both grades of primary schools are to be carried out under the supervision of the chief district administrative official. All private primary schools are conducted under the supervision of the same district authority.

Middle Schools

The object of the middle school is to complete the general education of the child and to produce efficient and all-round citizens. For the first time in Chinese history, middle schools for girls are specifically provided for, on the same basis as those for boys.[9] The establishment of middle schools is left to the provincial authorities. The governor of each province is ex-

---

[9] Middle schools for girls modeled after those for boys had existed before the revolution.

pected to decide the location and number of such schools required in his province and to report the same to the Minister of Education. The Minister of Education has, however, the right to order the various provinces to increase the number of middle schools whenever he deems it absolutely necessary. Provincial middle schools are to be built and maintained by the revenue of the provinces. In case the various districts, after having established the number of primary schools required by law, find themselves possessing financial strength to do more, they are permitted to establish, either singly or conjointly, middle schools which shall be known as district middle schools to distinguish them from the provincial middle schools. Private individuals or corporations are also allowed to establish middle schools which shall be known as private middle schools. In any case, the establishment, reorganization, or abolition of any middle school must first receive the sanction of the Minister of Education. Middle school teachers are to be chosen from those who have been recognized as possessing the necessary qualifications by the Association for the Examination and Certification of Teachers.[10] The salary of the principal and the teachers in middle schools is to be determined by the governor, in accordance with the standard established by the Ministry of Education. The amount of tuition charged by the middle school is to be determined by the head of the school concerned, in accordance with the standard drawn up by the Ministry of Education. If for some special reasons the required tuition is either to be reduced or to be entirely remitted, the sanction of the provincial authorities must first be secured. The amount of tuition charged by a private middle school is to be determined by the organizers of the school concerned, but a report must be made to the governor.

The University

The aim of the university is to impart higher learning with a view to training men of great ability for the use of the nation. The organization of the university differs from the one which existed before the revolution in that it has seven faculties instead of eight, having dropped the faculty of classics. The courses

[10] The date of enforcement of this requirement is to be fixed by separate ordinance. See Educational Ordinance No. 13, Art. 15, September 28, 1912.

now offered cover the following subjects: arts, science, law, commerce, medicine, agriculture, and applied science. The preparatory department has three groups of studies: the first is for those who wish to enter the faculties of arts, law. and commerce; the second for those who wish to enter the faculties of science, applied science, agriculture, and pharmacy; and the third for those who wish to enter the faculty of medicine. The period of post-graduate study is indefinite instead of limited to five years as was the case under the old system.

The alternative courses of the three preparatory years in the university are as follows:

First Group of Studies:

1. Foreign Languages	3. History	5. Psychology
2. Literature	4. Logic	6. Law

Elective studies: Political Economy, Mathematics, and Physics, to be chosen according to the course to be followed later.

Second Group of Studies:

1. Foreign Languages	4. Physics	7. Mineralogy
2. Literature	5. Chemistry	8. Drawing
3. Mathematics	6. Geology	

Elective studies: Zoölogy, Botany, Surveying, to be chosen according to the course to be followed later.

Third Group of Studies:

1. Foreign Languages	4. Mathematics	7. Zoology
2. Literature	5. Physics	8. Botany
3. Latin	6. Chemistry	

Two foreign languages are to be studied in each group. Those who expect to take courses in Agriculture, Applied Science, or Medicine, must study German.

The courses for the different schools of the university are as follows:

I. Arts:
  1. Chinese and Western Philosophy
  2. Literature
    a. Chinese
    b. Sanscrit
    c. English
    d. French
    e. German
    f. Russian
    g. Italian
    h. Philology
  3. History
    a. Chinese and Oriental in general
    b. Western
  4. Geography

II. Science:
  1. Mathematics
  2. Astronomy
  3. Theoretical Physics
  4. Experimental Physics
  5. Zoölogy
  6. Botany
  7. Geology
  8. Mineralogy

III. Law:
  1. Law
  2. Government
  3. Political Economy

IV. Commerce:
  1. Banking
  2. Insurance
  3. Foreign Commerce
  4. Consular System
  5. Customs Revenue
  6. International Law

V. Medicine:
  1. Medicine
  2. Pharmacology

VI. Agriculture:
  1. Agriculture
  2. Agricultural Chemistry
  3. Forestry
  4. Veterinary Science

VII. Applied Science:
  1. Construction Materials
  2. Machinery
  3. Machinery of Vessels
  4. Shipbuilding
  5. Military Science
  6. Electricity
  7. Building
  8. Industrial Chemistry
  9. Explosives
  10. Mining
  11. Minting

It is the plan of the government to found three new universities, one in Nanking, one in Wuchang, and one in Canton. In the meantime the Peking University is being reorganized.

Professional Schools

The object of these schools is to train for some special profession or vocation. They may be established by the central government, by the provincial authorities, or by private enterprise. Graduates of the middle schools or those with equal qualifications may be admitted. The classification of these schools is as follows:

1. Law
2. Medicine
3. Pharmacology
4. Agriculture
5. Commerce
6. Mercantile Marine
7. Art
8. Music
9. Applied Science
10. Languages

Normal Schools

Normal schools are divided into the following kinds: boys' normal school, girls' normal school, and higher normal school. The aim of the normal schools is to train elementary school teachers; that of higher normal school is to train teachers for the middle and normal schools. Normal schools, like middle schools, are to be established by the provinces. It shall be the duty of the governor to determine the location and number of schools required, and after making due report to the Ministry of Education to establish the schools as planned. For special reasons a district may, after receiving the sanction of the Ministry of Education through the provincial authorities, establish normal schools to be known as district normal schools. Two or more districts may likewise establish normal schools conjointly. Private individuals and corporations may also, after receiving the sanction of the Ministry of Education through the provincial authorities, establish normal schools. Higher normal schools are to be regarded as national institutions, and are to be established by the central government. The Minister of Education shall after due consideration of the need of the nation as a whole, determine the location and number of higher normal schools and have them established.

The expenditure for normal schools is to be met by the revenue of the provinces, and that for the provincial higher normal schools by the national treasury.[11] The salary schedule of normal school principals and teachers is determined by the governor, in accordance with the standard drawn up by the Ministry of Education.[12] All students of normal and higher normal schools shall be exempt from tuition. Each student shall also receive from his school an allowance large enough to cover the necessary expenses in the school. The normal schools are, however, permitted to receive students who prefer to be self-supporting.

An elementary school shall be attached to each normal school, and each higher normal school shall have one elementary school and one middle school attached to it. In the case of normal and higher normal schools for girls, besides the necessary elementary

[11] The date for the enforcement of this rule is yet to be determined by the Ministry. See Educational Ordinance No. 14, Art. 12, September 28, 1912.

[12] *Ibid.*

school and middle school, kindergartens shall be attached to them. Under special conditions a normal school may also conduct teachers' institutes for those who possess certificates to teach in elementary schools. In the case of girls' normal schools, special courses in practice teaching may also be offered to those who wish to become kindergarten teachers. Higher normal schools, both for boys and for girls, are permitted to organize special courses and also courses in investigation or research work.

The teaching positions in normal schools are to be filled only by those who have been recognized as possessing the necessary qualifications by the Association for the Examination and Certification of Teachers. The date for the enforcement of this rule has yet to be set by the Ministry.

Industrial Schools

It shall be the aim of the industrial school to impart the knowledge and skill required in agriculture, trades, and commerce. There shall be two kinds of industrial schools, A and B, the former giving a complete general industrial education, and the latter an elementary industrial education or training in special trades as demanded by local circumstances. Industrial schools include schools of agriculture, trades, and commerce, industrial continuation schools, and the like. Apprentice schools may be regarded either as trade schools of the elementary kind, or as trade continuation schools. Girls' trade schools similar to those for boys may be established if local conditions warrant.

Industrial schools of the A grade shall be established by the governor of the province; those of the B grade by districts, by cities, towns, or villages, or by bureaus of agriculture, trades, or commerce, but these may also be allowed to establish industrial schools of the A grade if local circumstances permit. The location of schools established by provinces and districts is determined by the governor and the district official respectively. Industrial schools are named by their source of support, such as provincial industrial schools, district industrial schools, and the like. The establishment, alteration, or abolishing of provincial industrial schools must be reported to the Minister of Education, but in the case of district industrial schools must receive the approval of the governor and then be reported by him to the Minister of Education. In the case of industrial continuation schools the only requirement is that a report be made to the governor. If local circumstances permit, the tuition required of industrial students may be remitted.

The New Curriculum

With the reorganization of the school system a new curriculum has been introduced which differs from that existing before the revolution, involving in more than one respect radical departures from the traditional standards. We shall make a brief examination of the curricula of primary schools, middle schools, and normal schools, noting a few of the more important changes that have been effected.

Curriculum of the Primary Schools

The course of study for the lower primary school continues to cover four years. The subjects required are as follows: morals, mother tongue, mathematics, hand-work, drawing, singing, and physical culture. One or more of the three last mentioned subjects may be temporarily dropped, in case of absolute necessity. Sewing is added to the program of girls. This course of study differs from the old one in several ways. Chinese classics, history, geography, and nature study, found in the old curriculum, have been left out. Hand-work is made compulsory instead of optional. The number of hours per week for the first year has been reduced from twenty-four to twenty-two, that for the second increased from twenty-four to twenty-six; and the number of weekly recitations for the third and fourth years has been reduced from thirty to twenty-eight for boys and twenty-nine for girls.[13]

The course of study for the higher primary school has been reduced from four to three years. The subjects to be taught are as follows: morals, mother tongue, mathematics, Chinese history, geography, physical science, hand-work, drawing, singing, and physical culture. Agriculture is added to the studies of boys, and sewing to those of girls. If local conditions demand, agriculture may be left out or be replaced by commerce, and English may be added to the curriculum. In case of absolute necessity, hand-work and singing may also be temporarily left

13 For full program of the lower primary school, see Appendix, Table I.

out, and English may be replaced by another foreign language. Special courses for making up deficiencies in school work may be offered. If a child is found physically unable to pursue a certain subject of study, he may be exempted from taking it. With the sanction of the chief of the local administrative officials, the subject matter of the curriculum may be increased or decreased to suit local conditions. This new course of study is conspicuous by the absence of Chinese classics which used to occupy one-third of the total number of school hours. It is also marked by a decrease in the number of recitations. Instead of thirty-six hours per week throughout the course, the first year now has only thirty hours and the second and third thirty for boys and thirty-two for girls.[14]

Curriculum of Boys' Middle Schools

The course of study for the middle school has been reduced from five to four years. In place of the two courses of the system introduced in 1909, only one course is now offered. This must be regarded as a step backward in that it does not seem to be in keeping with the modern tendency in secondary education, namely, to provide more diversified courses of study to meet the varying needs of pupils. The new curriculum prescribes the following subjects of study: morals, Chinese language, foreign language, history, geography, mathematics, nature study, physics, chemistry, government, economics, drawing, hand-work, music, and physical culture. This list differs from the one existing before the revolution in the absence of Chinese classics and the addition of hand-work, showing a victory of the more practical subject over the linguistic or the classical. The number of recitations per week is reduced from thirty-six throughout the course to thirty-three for the first year, thirty-four for the second, and thirty-five for the third and the fourth.[15] Under special circumstances the head of the boys' or girls' middle school may increase or reduce the number of hours for particular subjects in the various school years, but the total number of hours in a week should in no case be less than thirty-two, and in none more than thirty-six.

---

[14] For full program of the higher primary school, see Appendix, Table II.
[15] For full program of boys' middle schools, see Appendix, Table III.

Curriculum of Girls' Middle Schools

In the girls' middle schools household arts, gardening, and sewing are required, though gardening may be left out. English is used as the standard foreign language, but under special conditions one of the following languages may be selected in its place: French, German, and Russian. The number of recitations per week is thirty-two for the first year, thirty-three for the second, thirty-four for the third and the fourth, one hour less in each year being required than in the case of the boys' middle school.[16]

Curriculum of Boys' Normal Schools[17]

The new curriculum provides for the boys' normal school two courses of study, A and B, the former including a preparatory course of one year and a regular course of four years, the latter lasting one year. Course A in the boys' normal school requires the following subjects of study: ethics, education, Chinese language, writing, English, history, geography, mathematics, nature study, physics and chemistry, civics and economics, drawing, hand-work, agriculture, music, and physical culture. This list differs from the old one in the absence of Chinese classics and the addition of the following subjects of study: English, civics and economics, hand-work, agriculture, and music. Instead of having thirty-six hours per week as under the old system, the new curriculum prescribes for Course A the following number of hours: in the preparatory course thirty-two hours per week; in the regular course thirty-three for the first year, and thirty-five for each of the remaining three years. The subjects of study for Course B are as follows: ethics, education, Chinese literature, mathematics, nature study, physics and chemistry, drawing, hand-work, agriculture, music, and physical culture. The work occupies thirty-five hours per week.

Curriculum of Girls' Normal Schools[18]

The curriculum of the girls' normal school is similar to that of the boys' in having two courses, A and B, the former requiring four years following one preparatory year, and the latter being

[16] For full program of girls' middle schools, see Appendix, Table IV.

[17] For full program, see Appendix, Tables V and VI.

[18] For full program, see Appendix, Tables VII and VIII.

merely a short course of one year. The subjects of study in Course A differ from those of the boys' normal school in the omission of agriculture and the addition of household arts and gardening, and sewing. The number of recitations required is in each case slightly larger than that required in boys' normal schools, being thirty-three hours for the preparatory course, thirty-five for the first year of the regular course, and thirty-six for the second, the third, and the fourth year. However, the subject of English, requiring three hours per week, may be omitted if circumstances seem to warrant such action. When that is done, the number of hours per week becomes a little less than that required in the boys' normal schools, being thirty hours for the preparatory course, thirty-two hours for the first year of the regular course, and thirty-three hours for each of the remaining three years. Course B of girls' normal schools is the same as that of boys', with the exception that sewing is introduced in the place of agriculture, and that the girls have thirty-four hours per week, while the boys have thirty-five.

Curriculum of the Higher Normal Schools

The curriculum of the higher normal school is divided into three courses: the preparatory course, the regular course, and the research work. The preparatory course lasts one year, the regular course three years, while the research work may cover either one or two years. The subjects of study for the preparatory course are as follows: ethics, Chinese language, English, mathematics, drawing, singing, and physical culture. The regular course is taken in one of the following departments: (1) Chinese language; (2) English; (3) history and geography; (4) mathematics and physics; (5) physics and chemistry; and (6) nature study. Each department prescribes a number of studies forming a group by itself, but all the departments have the following subjects in common: ethics, psychology, education, English, and physical culture. The research course requires the intensive study of two or three subjects chosen from the departments of the regular course. Two other courses may be offered by higher normal schools, one providing for specialization and one elective course, each lasting from two to three years. The program of studies for the various courses of a higher normal school is drawn up by the principal of that school, but must be reported to the Minister of Education. This new curriculum of the higher normal school, like that of other schools, is conspicuous by the disappearance of classics as one of the required subjects of study, and by the presence of studies heretofore omitted.

Summary

Our examination of the new curricula reveals the fact that the changes made have been along three general lines: the elimination of Chinese classics as a subject in itself, the introduction of new subjects of study having a social and industrial significance, and the relief of the over-crowded program. The first change reduces largely the time formerly allotted to Chinese literature, thus making room for the more liberal introduction of western subjects which require the use of the laboratory or experimental method. The second change makes possible a closer adjustment of the school work to the changing social and industrial demands, and supplies the rising generation with an opportunity for sense-training and for the acquisition of skill through such studies as hand-work, drawing, domestic science, and agriculture. The last change tends not only to reduce superficiality in school work, but also to prevent an over-taxing of the physical strength of school children. Unquestionably these moves, being in keeping with the progressive ideas of modern education, are tending in the right direction and should be encouraged.

New Rules and Regulations

That the reorganization of the educational system has been most thorough in character is attested by the further fact that there have been put into force during the first two years of the life of the republic, various sets of new rules and regulations governing one or another phase of the school system, including those relating to school uniform, school ceremonies, transfer of pupils from one school to another, school government, school year, school term and vacations, school fees, student records, and text-books. A summary of the more important of these rules will be given here to complete the picture of the new school system.

School Government[19]

The spirit of school government reflects the nature of the political government. Under the monarchy, rules governing the school and student life were minutely laid down by the Ministry of Education and arbitrarily thrust upon the school authorities for enforcement. Since the establishment of the republic a more liberal spirit and policy have been introduced. The detailed regulations governing schools and student life are now left to be drawn up by heads of schools to accord with the type of school and with local conditions, though such regulations must be reported to the Ministry of Education in case of national schools and to local authorities in case of schools established by the local government or private individuals. The Ministry of Education now satisfies itself by prescribing one general rule that is required of all schools. No official provision is yet made for student participation in school government, with the exception of a statement to the effect that in case any student has suggestions to make relating to the instruction or the management of the school, he is allowed to present them to the proper school authorities either in writing or in person. Students are, however, permitted to organize clubs or societies to promote the welfare of body and mind, such as amusement clubs, musical clubs, physical culture clubs, and the like, but these organizations must receive the approval of the head of the school and be conducted under the supervision of the school authorities. One of the ways to insure obedience to school rules is the provision that students dismissed for violation of regulations are not allowed to enter another school unless they provide proper guarantee to show that they have really repented and reformed.

New School Year, Term, and Vacations[20]

The adoption of the Western calendar by the Republic of China naturally necessitated the creation of a new school calendar, in order to avoid inconsistency or incongruity. The new school year, which extends from August 1st to July 31st, is divided into three terms, the first term extending from August 1st to December 31st, the second from January 1st to March 31st, and the third from April 1st to July 31st. The summer vacation

---

19 Educational Ordinance No. 3, 1912.
20 Educational Ordinance No. 6, September 3, 1912.

may not be less than thirty days nor more than fifty days. This rule, however, does not apply to colleges and higher technical schools. Each school determines for itself the best time for its vacation after due consideration of the climatic conditions of the community. The New Year vacation is between seven and fourteen days in length. The length of the spring vacation is fixed at seven days, April 1st to 7th. Primary schools in the rural districts are free to shorten their New Year and summer vacations, and to close in spring and autumn during the sowing and harvesting seasons. In case they are obliged, for this reason, to open school in the summer, they must shorten their school hours. Schools situated in extremely cold regions are free to give winter vacations and to shorten their summer and spring vacations. All schools are closed on Sundays and memorial days.[21]

School Fees[22]

According to the standard set up by the Ministry of Education, the lower primary school should be free, but under special circumstances a monthly fee of thirty cents or less is permitted. It should be stated here that Chinese money approximates the Mexican standard, its dollar being about half the value of the American dollar. The fee charged by higher primary schools should not exceed one dollar a month, and that for supplementary courses should not exceed sixty cents a month. The fee of the elementary industrial school should never be higher than sixty cents per month. The monthly fee of the middle school ranges from one to two dollars, and that of higher industrial schools from eighty cents to one dollar and fifty cents. Professional schools charge a fee of from two dollars to two dollars and fifty cents a month. The tuition at the university is three dollars per month. Normal and higher normal schools both exempt students from paying any tuition, but at the time of admission a deposit of ten dollars or less is collected, which is returned at the time of graduation. The tuition of the lower and higher primary schools and industrial schools is paid monthly, while the tuition of the middle, industrial, and professional

---

[21] Memorial days include the anniversary of the establishment of the Republic, the birthday of Confucius, any local memorial days, and the anniversary of the school. *Ibid.*

[22] Educational Ordinance No. 15, 1913.

schools and of the university is paid once in each school term. School authorities have the right to remit either wholly or in part the tuition fees of poor students and of those who make the best record in school work, and to make other modifications, provided permission is received from either the local government or the Minister of Education.

School Records

All schools are required to keep at least two records of individual students, one of conduct and one of scholarship. The conduct record is to be kept under four grades: A, B, C, D. A student making a record of C or above is regarded as having reached the standard. To those meriting A the head of the school may issue a certificate of commendation. The student's records in conduct and scholarship are both taken into consideration in the determination of promotion or graduation. Those whose scholarship record falls below the standard by one-tenth but whose record of conduct is A or B are entitled to promotion or graduation. On the other hand, those whose record of conduct just meets the requirement and whose scholarship is ranked as D may be denied promotion or graduation. Such cases, however, must be discussed at the teachers' meeting before action is taken by the head of the school. Regulations relating to students' conduct in special schools may be drawn up by the head of the school in accordance with local conditions.

The scholarship record of the student is of two kinds, the daily record and the examination record. The daily record is based on the earnestness with which the student pursues his studies as well as the quality of his work. The examinations are of three kinds: term, annual, and graduation. In addition to these, there are also examinations of admission, of promotion, of enrollment, and of transfer from one school to another. In determining the scholarship record, four grades are to be used, A, B, C, D:

A	signifies	a	grade	above	80	per cent.
B	"	"	"	"	70	"
C	"	"	"	"	60	"
D	"	"	"	not up to	60	"

Grades above C are regarded as fulfilling the requirement; D is regarded as failure. Those reaching the standard are promoted or graduated; but those who do not reach the standard are retained in the same grade or class. Those failing twice to reach the standard are asked to withdraw from school. Detailed rules are laid down by the Ministry of Education as to how to compute or determine the pupil's record for the term, for the year, and for graduation.

Control of Text-Books[23]

Under the new conditions the preparation and publication of text-books and teachers' manuals are left entirely in the hands of private individuals, but as in the pre-revolutionary days all such books must receive the approval of the Ministry of Education before they are allowed to be used in schools. In each province there has been established a text-book commission charged with the duty of selecting, from the approved list of books drawn up by the Ministry of Education, such as are suitable to the conditions in the province and of recommending these to the school authorities for adoption. Minute rules regulating the certification of text-books and the organization of provincial text-book commissions have been promulgated and are being rapidly put into practice.[24]

---

23 Educational Ordinance No. 18, 1914.

24 For detailed information see Educational Ordinances, Nos. 9 and 10, 1912.

CHAPTER VII

PRESENT-DAY EDUCATIONAL PROBLEMS OF NATIONAL IMPORTANCE

The story of the origin, development, and reconstruction of the Chinese educational system, which we have attempted to record briefly in the preceding pages, has given rise to many problems of vital importance aside from those which have already received our attention. The factors involved in these problems are so numerous and their interrelations are so complex, that it is extremely difficult to suggest ways of solution which would be entirely satisfactory. Nevertheless, there are sufficient data at hand to warrant at least the mention of a few of the more important problems and to indicate some possible oluti ons.

Relation of Missionary Education to the Public Educational System

One of the problems of growing importance has to do with the educational work undertaken by missionaries from the West, both Catholic and Protestant. This work, inspired by evangelistic and philanthropic motives and begun in a humble way, has in recent years so developed in scope and character that it has come to exercise a considerable influence over the progress of new education in China. In the year 1912 there were in China under the various Protestant missions alone, 3,708 primary or day schools with 86,241 pupils enrolled and 5,537 intermediate and high schools with an enrollment of 31,384 pupils.[1] As many as thirty institutions have assumed the name of college, and nine of these have even adopted the name of university. Statistics of the educational work of the Catholic missionaries are not available, but it is generally known that it is not so highly developed as that of Protestants. The schools which they have established are the "prayer-schools" in which

1 China Mission Year Book, 1912.

the Christian children learn to read; normal schools for the training of catechists and Christians of higher standing; seminaries for the education of the Chinese clergy; and convents for the training of nuns. Certain missions in which there has grown up a Christan elite have opened for its benefit colleges which are nearly always under the direction of congregations of teaching brothers. A few years ago twin universities were created in Shanghai known respectively as the Dawn (Aurore) and the Morning Star (Etoile du Matin) [2] Statistics showing the combined educational force of the Protestant and Catholic missionaries are also not available, except that it has been roughly estimated that there are 100,000 pupils enrolled in the mission schools of China.[3]

The strong desire of the Chinese people for modern learning and the fact that the government of China has seriously undertaken to provide this education on a national basis, have begun to affect the status of missionary education in more than one way. To say the least, they have convinced the missionary body, as well as the home boards of foreign missions, of the necessity of reconsidering their educational policy and of placing their work on a firmer basis. As a result, various educational organizations, commissions, and committees have come into existence, and the subject of missionary education has received special attention in most of the important religious conferences and conventions held during the last few years. The aims of missionary education have been more clearly formulated; its results, defects, and causes of failure are being pointed out; and recommendations to meet the new demands have been strongly urged.[4] The importance of union and cooperation among the different denominations engaged in educational work, the necessity of unifying and standardizing the work of the different grades of schools, the need of avoiding wasteful overlapping and competition, and the desirability of having better teachers and other educational leaders, have been the cry of the day, and already steps have been taken to put into effect some of these timely and important suggestions.

---

[2] *The Chinese Recorder:* October, 1913, pp. 624–625.

[3] *The International Review of Missions:* October, 1912, p. 587.

[4] Cf. Report on Christian Education, American-Canadian Commission; Christian Education: World Missionary Conference, Vol III.

The question naturally arises: "What attitude should the Chinese government take toward missionary education, which is being strengthened and improved?" Under the Manchu dynasty graduates of missionary schools were debarred from receiving degrees and titles from the government, and the schools were not even asked to register. When the franchise for the election of representatives to the provincial assemblies was given to certain classes of people the graduates of government institutions were included, but not those of mission colleges. This discrimination was made, no doubt, on account of the desire of the government to preserve the national character of the new educational movement, and was neither anti-Christian nor anti-foreign, as it has sometimes been thought. The establishment of the republic has changed the whole situation, though thus far no definite action has been taken by the new government regarding the relation of missionary education to the governmental system. It was reported, however, that the Ministry of Education in 1912 sent a special deputy to Japan to study the method adopted there for recognizing the work of mission schools.

The question before us seems to involve at least three considerations: first, the sort of system of recognition and control which the government should adopt; second, the probable attitude of the missionary body toward such a system; and last, the advantage to the government of having such a system. In regard to the system of recognition and of control, the situations in Japan and India throw some light on the problem. In Japan there are three positions that a Christian school may hold in relation to the government.[5] The first is that of merely having government sanction to carry on a certain kind of educational work. This involves practically no regulation or inspection of the schools, and of course imposes no restriction on religious teaching. By the second form of recognition a school is ranked as giving an education of a certain government grade, and this recognition implies certain privileges and imposes certain conditions, but permits full religious freedom. The chief privileges are the postponement of military conscription, admission to the higher government schools, transfer to and from government middle schools, and the one-year volun-

[5] *The Chinese Recorder:* September, 1912, pp. 525-528.

tary military service after graduation. The chief conditions accompanying this form of recognition are that the curriculum of the school must, in the main, conform to that of the government middle schools; there must be two hundred and twenty days of teaching exelusive of examinations and holidays; certain records and examination papers must be kept for the inspection of the government; certain reports must be made; there must be a certain proportion of licensed teachers; the school buildings and grounds must conform to certain regulations; and the work of the school must always be subject to governmental inspection. The third form of recognition makes a school an integral part of the government sytem, subject to all the requirements and enjoying all the privileges of a regular government school. The advantage which this form of recognition has over the second is that in the eyes of the public it confers greater prestige. This form of recognition is given on condition that the school submit to the government regulation prohibiting religious teaching and religious services. The prohibition against religious teaching is, however, carried out with varying degrees of strictness, apparently according to the attitude of local officials. In most schools voluntary religious instruction classes are allowed at some time of the day either in or outside of the school buildings.

In India,[6] where the educational system consists of institutions organized by private initiative but aided by government grants, missionary schools, like other private schools, receive grants-in-aid if they are efficient in the secular instruction conveyed, whatever may be the arrangements for religious instruction. The provision regarding this question, as embodied in the educational dispatch of 1854, is that the amount and continuance of the assistance given will depend upon the periodical report of the inspectors. In their regular inspections no notice whatsoever shall be taken of religious doctrines which may be taught in any school, and their duty is strictly confined to ascertaining whether the secular knowledge conveyed is such as to entitle it to consideration in the distribution of the sum which will be applied to grants-in-aid.

The present condition in China seems to warrant the adoption of some system of recognition which requires the fulfilment of

[6] *The International Review of Missions:* July, 1912, pp. 393–411.

certain educational standards, but takes no account whatsoever of the religious teaching. In accordance with the expressed sentiments of certain missionary bodies, the scheme here suggested would be considered fair and just by the missionary body as a whole. Indeed, the attitude of some missionaries is that even the third form of the Japanese system is desirable, for it is claimed that a better class of students come to schools that have this form of recognition, and that they receive religious instruction gladly and heartily when attendance is voluntary, so that though the direct results may be less, they are not a forced, hot-house product, but are genuine and healthy. Experience also shows that the system does not interfere with religious influences, as the school can easily be kept Christian in tone by other channels than the classroom. Furthermore, whatever disadvantages may result from the restrictions that come with this form of recognition are far outweighed by the benefits which accompany it, such as increased efficiency, increased public confidence, and an enlarged opportunity for Christian education.[7]

The experience of Japan and India and the educational conditions in China all point with favor to the introduction of a system of recognition and control of missionary education. Such a step would be beneficial to China in more than one way. It would enable the government to exercise its legitimate control and supervision over the educational work of the missionaries as it does over other private educational institutions of the country. Through this control the government can utilize the schools and colleges supported by religious bodies to supplement the national educational work, which for some time to come will be handicapped by the lack of funds. It gives the government also an opportunity to see that missionary education not only really *educates* but educates in such a way that the graduates will be thoroughly Chinese in spirit, fully in sympathy with the best thought and feeling of their own country, and not creatures of a new kind, ill-adapted to the environment in which they must by force of circumstances live and work.[8]

---

[7] Christian Education: World Missionary Conference, Vol. III.

[8] Some missionaries as well as Chinese claim that a number of missionary schools have tended to denationalize the pupils. According to Reverend Timothy Richard, the secondary schools have all been so Western as to make the students almost foreigners in thought and habits and largely out of touch with native thought and feeling. Cf. Christian Education: World Missionary Conference. Vol. III. *The Chinese Recorder:*

Education and the Development of Moral Character

By far the most important of the present-day educational problems of China is how to make use of the school as an agency for the development of moral character in the rising generation of the new republic. Under the old system of education the classical literature formed the centre of the school curriculum. Since this literature is a treasure house of some of the noblest of human aspirations and since the themes around which it centres have to do with man's personal, domestic, and civic duties, the training which one receives in assimilating its content is highly moral in character. It is this training which has produced in the Chinese people some of the fine and stable qualities which have been the strength of the nation for many ages. With the breaking down of the traditional system of education and the introduction of new subjects of study into the school curriculum, the old classic learning with its moral teachings, though it has not been entirely cast aside, can no longer exert the strong influence which it once had. Those who have not lost sight of the ancient ethical ideal and who at the same time realize the present moral crisis, have been asking the question: "Whence will come the morality of tomorrow?" Is it possible to preserve under modern conditions, and in harmony with modern intellectual requirements, an ethical ideal, not only as lofty as that which pervaded the old system, but deepened and widened by the hidden moral foundations of western civilization? Some of the more conservative thinkers have become so alarmed as to advocate a return to the old paths, and the restoration of classical learning to the supreme place in the schools. Happily there are those who have the vision to see that the old order of things can never be restored, but that there are possibilities in the new educational system which, if utilized, will produce results of far-reaching moral influence.

Even during the period of transition, there was a manifest determination to give ethical instruction a prominent place in the curriculum. Series of text-books in ethics were produced, and were put into general use. These not only registered an enormous advance upon the old method of teaching even the youngest students to memorize the classics, but also aimed at holding up the ideal of the "superior man," as represented by Confucius, in pictures or parables suited to the grade of the student. Although not beyond criticism in matter and arrangement, these ethical text-books were on the whole admirable and well adapted to their purpose.

With the dawn of the new era ushered in by the establishment of the republic, there has come a renewed emphasis upon the importance of moral education in the new school system. Our attention has already been called to the fact that in accordance with the ordinance of the Ministry of Education, the chief aim of the new educational system is the development of morals, and that instruction in ethics still occupies a prominent place in the school curriculum. The one thing which Yüan Shih Kai repeats and emphasizes in his inaugural speech is morality (tao teh), which is understood by him to include loyalty, faith, steadiness, and respectability.[9] This renewed determination of the leaders of China to maintain an ethical ideal by setting up moral character as the ultimate aim of education, and by the retention of moral instruction as a specific subject is indeed fortunate and will no doubt work for the best interests of China.

But it must be observed that the effort to develop moral character need not be confined to giving formal instruction in ethics as a subject of the school curriculum. Other subjects of study can also be used effectually to deepen and ennoble the sentiments and impulses which ethical instruction specifically inculcates. Chinese literature, including fiction, romance, biography, and poetry, may have the highest value in forming the moral life of the pupil, if it is used not only to reach the intellect, but to touch the feeling and bring the pupil into sympathy with ideal characters, deeds, and aspirations. History, likewise, affords ample opportunities for the appreciative treatment of high ideals and motives at work in the affairs of men and for the manifestation of the essential factors in the upbuilding of character. In this way the teacher of history, as well as of literature, can fill the mind of the pupil with examples from which he may receive valuable influences for the formation of right principles of thought and action. But the oppor-

---

[9] For an explanation of the four constituent parts of morality, see Inaugural speech of Yüan Shih Kai, *Journal of the American Asiatic Association:* Vol. XIII, No. 11, pp. 327-328.

tunity of exerting moral influence does not end with history and literature, for if we allow moral ideals to permeate the school, every subject of the curriculum may be made to contribute its share of influence toward the moralization of the pupil.

Mere instruction in principles of right conduct, indeed, is by no means sufficient for the formation of a child's character, however helpful it may be. It is generally believed that morality of precept is of little value, that morality cannot be taught as a mere abstraction apart from real life. Other more effective factors in character building must be utilized and their importance emphasized, if education in China is to accomplish the task expected of it. One of these potent factors is the personality of the teacher. Experience shows that the character of the pupil can be greatly modified by the daily example and inspiration of a leader, wise, generous, and just, who unconsciously holds before each pupil an ideal self and points the way to its realization. Teaching by example is more effective than teaching by precept. Another factor is found in the instincts and impulses of the pupil. A wise teacher will see that they find expression in good conduct and in the formation of desirable habits so that these may become permanent parts of the child's character. It is said that direct ethical teaching, tales of heroic deeds, soul-stirring fiction that awakens sympathetic emotions, may accomplish but little unless in the child's early life regard for the right, little acts of heroism, and deeds of sympathy are cultivated, unless the ideas and feeling find expression in action and so become a part of the child's being. We learn to do, not by knowing alone, but by knowing and doing. Educational leaders in China no doubt realize the importance of the factors here suggested, and will in time see that opportunities for the proper expression of right instincts and impulses are amply provided for in the school. Something has already been done in the way of encouraging athletic sports as well as various school activities that have a social significance. This is in the right direction, but such efforts should be multiplied and their importance in the formation of good habits and character must be more clearly stated and more strongly emphasized.

School Discipline and Government

Perhaps no phase of the Chinese modern educational system has been more adversely criticised than that relating to school discipline and government. For years after the adoption of the new educational system the student body was noted for its spirit of independence and unruliness. School riots and school strikes of one kind or another were of frequent occurrence. This unwholesome tendency to insubordination on the part of the students was sometimes attributed to their subverted conception of liberty and equality and sometimes to the peculiar nature of the student body, which often included persons quite advanced in age and thought. Such men came to school with ideas more or less formed and with a certain sense of personal pride which resented everything which they regarded as either encroaching upon their liberty or lowering their dignity. The fact that Chinese students as a class have been intensely nationalistic in spirit and eager to make their influence felt has also been responsible for some of the troubles. Moved by patriotism they seized every political crisis to hold mass meetings for the discussion of ways and means to meet the situation. Sometimes they sent telegraphic messages to the government counseling it as to how to solve particular problems of the state, often they went so far as to protest against the action of the government. Such behavior naturally was not encouraged by the authorities and in the attempt to suppress these outbursts of feeling, no small amount of friction was caused, and much trouble ensued.

This state of affairs was partly responsible for the poor discipline of the schools, but in many cases the cause of the troubles lay not so much in the students as in the inability of the school officials to cope with the situation through want of authority, lack of administrative ability, or unwillingness to use effective means owing to personal or other reasons.

Not infrequently the source of trouble was in the teaching body itself. Many of the teachers coming from the old school were not very sympathetic in their dealings with the students. They were too overbearing and haughty in spirit and presumed upon their authority by riding roughshod over the opinions of the students. On the other hand there were others who were too slack in establishing and maintaining discipline because they were either ignorant of their responsibility or indifferent to it. In short, many of the teachers were unprepared both in mind and in spirit for the work of teaching.

The problem of school discipline, however, is no longer so serious as it used to be. The troubles seem to be largely transitory in nature and characteristic of the period when necessary readjustments must be made, new relationships formed, and new standards of right and wrong set up. Indeed, a great change for the better has taken place during the last few years. The type of students now in school is much better than that of five years ago. There is not only a general manifestation of good discipline in the institutions, but the erroneous idea of liberty and equality seems to be fast disappearing. The students are now less inclined to dictate terms to the government in the matter of politics. They seem to realize that students, after all, are students, and that as students they are not full-fledged citizens and have no voice in practical politics. This change for the better is generally attributed to two causes: first, those entrusted with the management of schools have been given greater power in their sphere; and, second, there has been an influx into the schools of a higher type of teachers and administrative officers, who have not only devoted years to the special study of education, but who also possess truer and higher ideals of life. There is every reason to believe, therefore, that the problem in question will sooner or later be eliminated.

Meanwhile, something fundamental should be undertaken in order to remedy the evil at an early date. Greater care should be taken in placing men at the head of schools. Only men of administrative ability and strong character should be secured to act as principals. These should be given all the authority rightly attached to the office. Better teachers should be trained and their service utilized. In addition, the number of school activities which tend to develop in students the virtue of self-control and the habit of observing order should be multiplied. Above all, a greater degree of cooperation should be developed not only between the faculty and the higher authorities, but also between students and school officers. Some form of self-government which would give the students opportunity to participate in all affairs affecting the order and government of the school should be widely introduced. Care, however, must be taken to see that such attempts are not made in too abrupt a manner. Experience in America shows that where this method has been adopted as a remedy for the effects of poor discipline, or unwise management, it has usually failed.[10] If the restraints of external control are too suddenly removed and a school is thrown back upon itself without some preparation for self-government, the strain is apt to be too great and disaster ensues. This explains the reason why the transition from entire control by the teacher to government by the students, must be gradual and wisely directed to overcome the tendency to license or anarchy. Success in introducing such schemes of self-government is also dependent upon a clear recognition on the part of the school authorities and the students of their respective spheres of influence. The former should realize the limit of their own dominion of control, and the latter should be willing to respect and obey the legitimate authority of teachers and administrative officers.

The Financing of the New Educational System

The problem of financing the new educational system has been a matter of extreme difficulty. Under the old system of education all that was needed was sufficient funds to defray the expenses of the competitive examination system and to support the few colleges that were found in large cities. With the introduction of the modern system of education there was suddenly created a demand for an outlay greatly out of proportion to the funds available under the old regime. In order to carry out the new educational policy buildings had to be secured and furnished, teaching materials and text-books provided, and teachers who have had sufficient preparation employed. Under the old system all the government needed to do was to provide educational facilities for a few; now the plan is to extend education to all. To meet the heavy expense which this changed policy of education entails is therefore a difficulty well nigh insurmountable.

The ways and means by which the government launched the new system are full of interest to those who are concerned with the administration of education. Briefly, the funds for the

[10] Dutton and Snedden: Administration of Public Education in the United States, p. 514.

maintenance of the educational policy were included as one of the regular items of the national and provincial budgets. The sources of revenue for educational purposes were various. The statistical report of the Ministry of Education for 1910 classified the various incomes under the following items: (1) Income from public property; (2) interest from deposits; (3) governmental appropriations; (4) public funds; (5) tuition and fees; (6) compulsory contribution; (7) voluntary contributions; and (8) miscellaneous sources of income.[11] The ways by which some of these items of money were raised are extremely interesting and at times pathetic. In many instances the old colleges were converted into modern schools. Oftentimes the money formerly devoted to religious processions, theatrical exhibitions, and clan ancestral halls was put into the school fund. For a time temples and monasteries of the Buddhists and Taoists were converted into schools, and temple lands and incomes were appropriated to educational purposes. Official recognition was given to encourage private munificence. Frequently private gifts of large amount were made even without the solicitation of officials or the hope of reward. The enthusiasm for education also found expression in great personal sacrifices and even in martyrdom. The cases of such heroic devotion and self-sacrifice in the cause of education, if collected, would fill volumes of pathetic reading, and would reflect the wonderful devotion of the Chinese people to ideals. Some of the provinces increased the rate of certain local taxes, but such increases are said to have been generally small. In the Province of Hunan alone has there been a considerable surplus of money derived in this way at the disposal of the educational authorities.[12] Since the establishment of the republic the practice of increasing the rate of local taxes for educational purposes has become more general, but as yet no system of general taxation has been evolved.

The solution of the problem of financing the new educational system is dependent upon the larger problem of the national revenue system. Thus far the fiscal aspect of China's national life has been far from satisfactory. Under the Manchu regime financial matters were often controlled by unscrupulous officials,

---

11 Reinsch, Paul S.: Intellectual and Political Currents in the Far East, pp. 206-208.
12 Statistical Report of the Ministry of Education, 1910.

and the markets of China were frequently swept by devastating tides of financial insolvency which shook the foundation of many colleges and schools and threatened collapse. The revolutions which came in succession also played havoc with China's finances, and some years must elapse before their effect upon the balance of the government's revenue and expenditure ceases to be felt. It has been estimated that the first revolution alone cost China in additional public expenditures and private losses a sum of about taels 230,000,000 aside from the complete cessation of internal revenue for several months.[13] It is no wonder that during the last few years national deficits have been incurred and internal and foreign loans have been necessary. The financial chaos has been intensified by the fact that the financial system itself has been out of order owing to the inability to discriminate between the government tax and local tax and also to the conflict between the central and the provincial government. The local government at times fails to send its tax to the provincial government; while the provincial government often tries to send to the central government as little as possible of its collected taxes. Happily an earnest effort is being made to reorganize the national as well as the provincial system of finance with a view to placing them on a sounder basis.[14]

In the meantime the matter of financing the new educational system remains as one of China's unsolved problems. Under such circumstances two immediate steps might be taken. One is to avoid all unnecessary expenditure. This would mean that educational funds should be in no wise misappropriated; that the number of non-teaching offices which are mere sinecures must be reduced, or better still, entirely eliminated; that no expensive apparatus should be bought until the teacher and students who can make use of it are secured; and that no extravagance in the erection and furnishing of buildings should be permitted. The second step is to encourage private initiative. This means that private schools should be encouraged, that the old-style schools be reformed or improved through a system of awards and other devices, and that every effort put forth in China by the educators of the West should be given

[13] China Year Book, 1913, p. 305.

[14] *Republican Advocate*, Vol. II, No. 16, p. 635; also Vol. I, No. 27, p. 1145.

some form of recognition and their work placed under the control of the Chinese government. By these means the financial gap may be bridged over until China's revenue system is improved and her natural resources are developed. There is no occasion, however, for one to become discouraged at the seeming hopelessness of the financial situation of the country, for the natural resources of China are in no wise inferior to those of the richest of the western nations. They are only waiting to be developed. Yüan Shih K'ai in his inaugural speech compared the condition in China to that of the rich man who has buried his riches under the ground, and is complaining all the time of poverty. The reasons given by him as to why the industries of the country have not been developed are that the education of the country is still in its infancy and that large capital is not available. But with the development of modern education in the sciences and with the growing utilization of foreign capital one can reasonably expect that in the course of a decade the financial condition will be greatly improved.

Universal Education

The idea of education for all classes, the aim of all educators and statesmen of western countries, scarcely entered the minds of the leaders of China under the traditional system of education. With the introduction of the new educational system, however, the problem of universal education suddenly came into prominence. Indeed, it is the stated goal of the new educational policy. Thus far the attempt to furnish educational facilities for the masses has been only partially successful. In 1909, only one person in two hundred, or about one fortieth of the children of school age in the province of Chili, attended the government schools, while in Szechuan the proportion was one person in two hundred and seventy-five or one-fiftieth of the school population. Since then some advance has been made. The educational report of Kuangtung for the year 1912 states that forty per cent of the boys and thirteen per cent of the girls between the ages of six and nine were in school that year.

This problem of education for China's millions is fraught with difficulties. To begin with, there is the difficulty of the language, which is without an alphabet, so that learning to read is a much harder task than in most countries. This trouble is intensified by the fact that the written language is not the one spoken, and that the spoken language itself is not the same all over the country. Owing to the cumbersome vehicle of expression which China has, the time required for gaining a thorough education is lengthened by three to five years. During recent years various means of overcoming this difficulty have been proposed, the following being most significant: (1) to do away with mechanical memorizing and to substitute in its place the more rational process of teaching the meaning along with the characters; (2) to publish books and papers in colloquial characters, which are specially adapted to the daily speech of the people and easily understood; (3) to simplify words and methods of expression; (4) to teach Mandarin, the most universally spoken Chinese language, in the schools; (5) to use readers for teaching the Chinese language; (6) to introduce a phonetic language. Some of these have been tried out with varying degrees of success; some are still under discussion. Besides the difficulty of language there are the difficulties of supplying the system with a sufficient number of trained teachers and providing the revenue to maintain it. It is estimated that to make education anything like universal, China réquires one million schools in place of fifty thousand or more, which is the approximate number now, i. e., a multiplication by twenty or an addition of some nine hundred and fifty thousand schools having a staff of one million and a half to two million of teachers, with all that is involved in the preparation of these teachers and the financing of the scheme.

Since the establishment of the republic the problem of universal education has loomed large in the minds of Chinese statesmen and educators. Preliminary steps are being taken by the Ministry of Education to enforce under penalty the compulsory education laws requiring all children between the ages of seven and fourteen to attend school. Great emphasis is now being laid on primary education, and some adjustments and combinations are also being made in higher education, the money saved in the latter instance to be devoted to the establishment of more primary schools of both grades in order to hasten universal education. It has often been said that in introducing modern educational institutions, China made the mistake of starting at the top and building downwards, overlooking in her anxiety for universities, high schools, and middle schools, the great importance of primary schools. Assuming this charge to be true, the mistake is now being remedied, and primary education is receiving the attention which it deserves.

Training of Teachers

The difficulty of finding a sufficient number of competent teachers has been one of the greatest impediments to the progress of modern education in China. At the very outset the government and the people adopted and created the material forms and forces of modern education such as school houses, apparatus, maps, and the like, which were often ample and impressive, but the authorities were not able to supply these schools with a sufficient number of properly trained teachers. This condition of affairs does not mean that the government failed to take proper account of the problem, leaping in the dark, as it were, into the work of introducing modern education. It is rather to be explained by the fact that it is easy to set up a school but it is hard to train a teacher. Teachers cannot be made on short notice, though a school house can. They must be in a sense grown, and growth, unlike manufacturing, takes much time. Consequently, while there were school houses and pupils in abundance there was a dearth of teachers. The guns were made and mounted, so to speak, but there were not sufficient gunners to fire them. The rapid growth of the new educational system since its inception has made the problem of supplying the modern schools with competent teachers increasingly more difficult to solve.

The facts that China went into this work of educating a quarter of the population of the globe without a sufficient body of teachers and that the growth of the new educational system has been probably more rapid than was anticipated, would not have made the problem of supplying teachers so serious had China been able to recruit teachers from the old schools. This she has not been able to do, although many of the old teaching staff did find their way into modern schools. Chinese scholars there were, and many of them too, but they lacked the knowledge and the skill demanded of the teachers of modern schools. Under the old educational system any one could set up as a school teacher, and a great many scholars who had attained the first degree in the examination, to say nothing of the host of others who had failed, made this their chief means of obtaining a living. No certificate was required for teaching, and no book or curriculum was compulsory, except that which was universally established by tradition or usage. The instruction was usually imparted either in the home of the children or in that of the teacher. Such private schools seldom comprised more than twenty children. The kind of teaching tended to develop memory rather than reasoning power. Under the new system of education, the situation which the teacher has to face is entirely different. He must know more than mere Chinese classics and composition. He has to teach students in classes instead of individually. Again, the teacher in a modern school is expected to develop in the pupils the power of reasoning instead of only mere memory. And the old-style teacher does not easily lend himself to the new order. He is by training conservative, inclined to cling to the methods to which he is accustomed. He is himself so wedded to the old that he confesses to a sort of intellectual awkwardness when he tries to use the new learning and new methods. In his fear of making mistakes, he confines himself closely to text-books. Consciously or unconsciously he still over-emphasizes the value of memory. He himself is not trained to think and of course is not inclined to adopt methods which quicken thought in his student. Modern pedagogy is to him so new a science that either he has little appreciation of its worth, or, if he is able to appreciate, he is not able to use it with facility and efficiency.

Under such circumstances, the Chinese government and the people lost no time in resorting to various means to secure proper teachers to meet the urgent demand. The most available source of teachers able in a way to meet the new situation was the graduates of the missionary schools which we have already mentioned as the pioneers of modern education in China. At the time when the new education was coming in on a large scale, some of the better higher institutions managed by missionaries had turned out many graduates more or less fitted to assume the responsibility of modern teaching. It was but natural that they were sought by the governmental as well as the private schools. But the supply of teachers furnished by missionary schools and colleges was far from being adequate, as the demand was not only unusually great but was also constantly increasing in amount and in urgency.

The second source of recruiting teachers for modern schools in China was the ranks of the literati, many of whom, aware of their uselessness in the altered conditions of society, have tried to keep abreast of the times by acquiring modern knowledge through a more or less hasty perusal of books, but this method can give at best only imperfect and superficial information. To many of these men, modern education is a thing which can be gained by a short-cut; specialization, a thing which can be undertaken without the necessity of grasping the fundamental principles of knowledge. This type of men, whom we may call *amateur educators*, was attracted to the teacher's occupation under various circumstances and with various motives. Some entered it under purely philanthropic or patriotic impulse, and others took it up from economic considerations. While these amateurs represent as a whole a more desirable class than the old-style school teachers, by reason of their more progressive ideas and greater earnestness of purpose, yet it is plain that it would be a hazardous thing to entrust children to such guidance in the training which practically decides their life career.

When the system was first inaugurated it was necessary to secure foreign teachers, especially for the higher institutions, beginning with the middle and higher schools. The number of such teachers has never been very large, partly because comparatively few higher institutions of learning have been opened, and partly because the expense involved is much greater. The total number of foreigners employed in 1911 in the schools and colleges of all the provinces, including the metropolis, was 545.[15] There were twenty-one foreigners in the service of the College of Law in Peking and the Peking University engaged five professors of law, eight of science and engineering, three of agriculture, one of commerce, and four teaching in preparatory class of the university. The Tsing Hua College in Peking had eighteen American teachers, of whom nine were women.[16] For a time teachers from Japan were preferred partly because of their familiarity with the Chinese written language, and partly on the ground of economy since the salary was usually smaller and the necessary travelling expenses were also less; but this condition is no longer true.

---

15 China Year Book, 1913, p. 392.
16 Tsing Hua College: Bulletin of Information, No. 1.

The qualifications of foreign teachers have been varied. Some of them had had wide experience in educational work in China and were sincere in their desire to help China in her effort to develop a new educational system. On the other hand, there were men who not only had no love for teaching, but who were entirely ignorant of the rudimentary principles of education. These men found their way into the schools through the casualness or carelessness with which foreign teachers were once picked up. For during the early years the employment of foreign teachers was left entirely in the hands of individual institutions, and no uniform method or policy was adopted. It often happened that teachers were employed solely on the recommendation of some interested person or organization. They were employed and dismissed frequently, as the management of the school passed from one authority to another. Furthermore, it not infrequently happened that foreign instructors were engaged to teach special or advanced subjects which no students were ready to undertake. The result was that those specially qualified teachers had to spend a large portion of their time in teaching foreign languages or elementary subjects of study, instead of the subjects for which they were engaged. This state of affairs was brought to an end in 1908, when the Ministry of Education, with the approval of the Throne, put into force a set of rules according to which no foreign teachers could be employed in any of the modern schools of China without the sanction of the Ministry of Education. In case of military instructors the approval of the Ministry of War was necessary in addition to that of the Ministry of Education.

The fourth source of teachers was the returned students from abroad. The number of teachers so recruited has been comparatively small; especially is this true with respect to students returned from America and Europe. The chief reason for this state of affairs is that such students were urgently demanded in governmental and business positions which offer liberal remuneration. Even those who did find positions in schools rarely expected to devote their lives to teaching, but regarded it simply as a stepping stone to more lucrative employment. Indeed, it was observed a few years ago that even students especially sent out to be prepared for the profession of teaching were often drafted into other departments of the government instead of remaining in the service for which they had spent years of preparation. With a view to remedying this evil, the Ministry of Education in 1908 passed a law which required all students sent out by the Ministry of Education to teach at least five years upon their return to China. Before the completion of this required term of service no other department of the government can take them away to fill other positions. The strict enforcement of some such law, aided by sufficient remuneration and reasonably long tenure of office, should enable China to secure and retain permanently the services of men who have received thorough training as administrators and teachers in higher institutions of learning, as commissioners of education, inspectors of schools, or members of the boards of education, both national and provincial.

By far the largest number of teachers were found among graduates of Chinese normal schools and teachers' training schools. The new law requires, as did the old, that the graduates of normal schools should, after completing the course of study, devote themselves for a number of years to the work of teaching. The length of service varies according to the kind of training received. Any graduate of a normal school refusing to render such service is required to pay back as a fine the whole or a part of the cost of his education.[17]

Thus far the number of teachers trained has not equaled the number of teachers needed in different types of schools. The reason given by the Ministry of Education for this deficit is that in order to anticipate the yearly need of teachers one must know the statistics of the population, but such statistics have not been available. Consequently, it is impossible for the educational authorities to estimate the appoximate number of children of school age for each year and plan to train the required number of teachers. In 1911 the Ministry of Education informed the different provinces that the increase of the number of normal students should correspond to the increase in the number of elementary schools, and this was really the first step toward ensuring the training of the required number of normal students. Since the establishment of normal schools there has been a large number of graduates, most of whom had

[17] For further information regarding the length of service required and the repayment of the cost of education, see Educational Ordinance No. 34.

taken short and special courses, rather than full courses. In spite of the fact that some are of the opinion that there is now an excess of normal graduates, the facts given below prove that the number of teachers who have received a professional training is far from being sufficient.

During 1910 there were in China, excluding the missionary schools and those private schools which were not recognized by the government, 415 normal and teachers' training schools with 28,572 students enrolled. The following tables show the geographical distribution of schools and students as well as the number of students enrolled in the several courses of the various schools.

DISTRIBUTION ACCORDING TO PROVINCES

Province	*Schools*	*Students*	*Province*	*Schools*	*Students*
Chili	28	2,040	Kiangsi	17	887
Mukden	33	1,894	Hupeh	17	1,702
Kirin	7	470	Hunan	16	1,961
Heilungkiang	4	236	Szechuan	38	2,173
Shantung	16	1,283	Kuangtung	9	1,003
Shansi	17	812	Kuangsi	13	1,467
Shensi	10	580	Yunnan	18	1,140
Honan	62	3,818	Kweichow	9	726
Kiangning	19	2,000	Fukien	8	641
Kiangsu	5	493	Kansu	36	791
Anhui	19	1,093	Singkiang	1	143
Chekiang	13	1,219			
			Total	415	28,572

DISTRIBUTION ACCORDING TO COURSES

	Schools	*Students*
Higher Normal		
Full course	8	1,504
Elective course	14	3,154
Special course	8	691
Lower Normal		
Full course	91	8,358
Short course	112	7,195
Teachers' Training Schools	182	7,670
Total	415	28,572

The number of students in normal and teachers' training schools during the seven years 1903–1910, was as follows:

Year	*Higher Normal*	*Lower Normal*	*Teachers' Training Schools*
1903..............	....	80	.....
1904..............	....	1,500	90
1905..............	974	2,234	2,113
1906..............	1,069	5,031	2,088
1907.......	2,389	18,253	10,041
1908............. .	3,890	27,474	13,583
1909..............	5,817	19,383	12,819
1910..............	5,349	15,553	7,670

It appears from the above table that the number of students in lower normal and teachers' training schools reached its highest point in 1908, and then began to decrease; but that the number of students in the higher normal did not reach its highest till one year later, and that the decrease thereafter is not marked as in the case of the other schools. This phenomenon may be attributed to two causes. The first is that many of the schools established in a wave of enthusiasm were not fully prepared to meet the expense involved, and the result was that they soon went out of existence. Those which survived were in most cases better situated, financially and otherwise. The second cause is that in the course of the last few years there have been graduated from these schools, especially from the short and special courses, a sufficient number of teachers to staff the schools already established, and hence the demand for teachers of that type is not so urgent as in former years; moreover, most of those who expect to teach now prefer to take full courses instead of short and special courses, which were very popular in the early years of the development of education in China. In fact, the Ministry of Education issued orders to the effect that beginning in 1910 no more students should be admitted to the special course of the higher normal and the short course of the lower normal schools, for the alleged reason that there had already been a sufficient number of men graduated to fill positions of teachers in elementary schools. However, since the establishment of the republic short courses lasting one or two years have been introduced in normal schools and the establishment of special institutions offering similar courses for the training of rural teachers, has been authorized.

In view of the heterogeneous training of the men from whom the modern schools of China had to recruit their teachers, the necessity of providing some system to prevent the unqualified from making their way into the teaching corps soon became manifest. In 1909 the Ministry of Education issued regulations governing the certification of teachers for elementary schools. In the following year a system for the certification of teachers in lower normal and middle schools was adopted. According to the provisions of these two systems, the power of certifying teachers was in the hands of the Metropolitan Board of Education in case of Peking, or in the hands of the Commissioners of Education in case of the provinces. In order that teachers for elementary schools in districts far away from the provincial capital might be more conveniently certified, the Commissioner of Education had the power to appoint special officers to represent him. It was specifically stated in the regulations that the men appointed for the certification of teachers should be educational officers thoroughly familiar with the method and principles of education and possessing a good education and high respectability. For the certification of teachers for elementary schools, the examiners had to be teachers of special subjects, graduates of complete courses in higher normal schools, or graduates of institutions which have the standing of the high school. Those appointed for the certification of teachers for lower normal and middle schools had to be well-known and well-educated teachers of higher normal schools and technical schools of high rank, or graduates of Chinese and foreign high schools and colleges, who had had some experience in educational work.

Under the republic a new system of certifying teachers has been adopted, although it has not yet been put into practice. According to this new system all primary teachers must possess a teaching certificate. To obtain this certificate one must be a graduate of either a normal school or other schools designated by the Minister of Education or must be a person whose qualification to teach has been recognized by an association to be organized in the provinces known as Chien Ting Wei Yüan Hui, meaning the association of officers charged with the duty of selecting and certifying teachers. The new system also requires that all teachers in normal schools should possess certificates showing recognition by the same association as being qualified to teach in such schools.

From what has been said it seems clear that the present teaching staff of China is a conglomerate class, consisting of graduates of mission schools, graduates of governmental, public, and private schools giving a general education, returned students from abroad, teachers from the old Chinese schools, amateur teachers, foreign teachers, and graduates of normal and teachers' training schools. The statistical report of the Ministry of Education for the year 1910 indicates that during that year there were in the modern schools of China 89,766 teachers, as against 73,703 for 1909, and 63,566 for 1908, showing a marked increase in the teaching staff. Of these teachers, 84,755 were in schools of general culture, 2,712 in technical and vocational schools, and 2,299 in normal and teachers' training schools. The character of the qualification of this teaching body can be gained from the following statistics:[18]

1. SCHOOLS OF GENERAL CULTURE

a. MIDDLE SCHOOLS

Qualification	*Number*	*Percentage*
Graduates of normal schools	848	25.82
Graduates of schools other than normal	1,260	38.35
Foreigners	91	2.79
Non-graduates and those who have not attended modern schools	1,087	33.04
Totals	3,286	100.00

b. HIGHER PRIMARY

Graduates of normal schools	6,867	40.20
Graduates of schools other than normal	3,172	18.57
Non-graduates and those who have not attended modern schools	7,005	41.01
Foreigners	36	.22
Totals	17,080	100.00

c. LOWER PRIMARY—KINDERGARTEN

Graduates of normal schools	33,348	51.90
Non-graduates of normal schools	30,978	48.10
Totals	64,326	100.00

18 Statistical Report of the Ministry of Education, 1910.

2. Normal Schools

a. higher normal

Qualification	*Number*	*Percentage*
Graduates of modern schools in China	152	32.55
Graduates from schools abroad	144	30.84
Non-graduates and those who have not attended modern schools	80	17.13
Foreigners	91	19.48
Totals	467	100.00

b. lower normal

Graduates of normal schools	523	41 80
Graduates of courses other than normal	353	28.10
Non-graduates and those who have not attended modern schools	349	27.90
Foreigners	27	2.20
Totals	1,252	100.00

c. teachers' training

Graduates of normal schools	334	57.58
Graduates of courses other than normal	126	21.73
Non-graduates and those who have not attended modern schools	116	20.00
Foreigners	4	.69
Totals	580	100.00

3. Technical

Graduates of modern schools in China	397	32.30
Graduates from schools abroad	370	31.70
Non-graduates and those who have not attended modern schools	297	25.50
Foreigners	122	10.50
Totals	1,168	100.00

4. Vocational

Graduates of modern schools	748	48.20
Graduates from schools abroad	243	15.50
Non-graduates and those who have not attended modern schools	445	28.95
Foreigners	108	7.35
Totals	1,544	100.00

Several facts in regard to these figures need emphasis. First, the percentage of foreign teachers is greater in higher institutions than in lower; second, comparatively few of the graduates of modern schools have had any professional training; third, there is a large percentage of teachers who either have never attended any modern schools themselves or who have not graduated. This last class includes all sorts of unemployed men who considered teaching in the schools as a bed of roses, an attractive opportunity to do a few hours of work and draw a large salary. These facts go to show that the teaching corps of the modern schools of China was, in 1910, far from being competent and professional in character. In consequence of this state of affairs the incompetency of the teachers in some schools was most glaring. Some leading educators in China are of the opinion that even the earlier graduates of normal schools in China have proved for the most part unsatisfactory. This criticism, if true, is not surprising. Most of the young men who attended the normal schools had not had the mental training of primary and secondary schools as a basis for more advanced work. Moreover a large number of subjects in the normal schools were taught in a superficial manner owing to the overcrowding of courses of study which necessarily led to sham and cram and also to physical weakness or inefficiency. Considering the facts that the full course is now becoming popular with normal students, that the number of recitations per week is being reduced, and that more and more of those who enter the normal school will be graduates of primary and middle schools of the modern type, it is but reasonable to expect that from now on a better class of normal graduates will be turned out into the teaching service.

Relating Education to Life

There is at least one more educational problem of importance deserving special mention, namely, the problem of effectively relating education to the life of those who receive it. In the western countries the conflict so long waged between formal book training and the newer, more practical forms of education centering in the social and industrial needs of children, may be said to have been settled theoretically, at least, in favor of the latter, but in China this conflict has only just begun.

For not until recent years has there been felt the need of bringing about a closer adjustment of school work to the changing social and industrial demands of the time and of making the curriculum a means of preparing the pupils to solve the problems of their daily life. True enough, most of the modern school subjects such as geography, civics, and the like, have been introduced into the regular course of study, but these subjects are often taught without much reference to the daily life of the pupil or that of the community. As a result, a serious doubt has arisen in the minds of many of the Chinese as to the efficacy of modern education in solving the perplexing problems of the country. There is a feeling on the part of some that both the subjects taught in school and the method used in teaching those subjects do little good to the children. Indeed, a loud cry has already been raised against this form of education as failing to do what is expected of it.[19] The charge is made that from the moment a child enters school, he begins to alienate himself from the life of the family and that of the community, and by the time he graduates he is fit neither to be a farmer nor to be a merchant. This serious charge against new education, although it is not true of all schools, is yet not made without grounds. The root of the trouble lies, as already suggested, in the fact that much of the school work consists of merely imparting knowledge without reference either to the purposes which brought the children to school, or to the needs of the community in which they live. To remedy the evil something fundamental needs to be done both in the selection of material for the curriculum and in the method of teaching the various subjects of study. Fortunate it is for the new republic that these two problems are beginning to receive the serious attention of her more progressive leaders in education.

---

[19] Mr. Huang Yen Pei, the commissioner of education of the province of Kiangsu, published in the fall of 1913 a pamphlet in which he disclosed some startling facts regarding the character of the work done in some schools, and made a strong plea for a more practical form of education.

CHAPTER VIII

SUMMARY AND CONCLUSIONS

The development of the Chinese system of public education having been traced through its many vicissitudes, and a more or less critical study of a few of the important educational problems of to-day having been presented, there remains the need for a summarized statement of some of those facts revealed by the study which have a significant bearing upon the future progress of education in China.

Education and National Progress[1]

The history of Chinese education forms an excellent example of the important relation of school training to national progress. For many centuries Chinese education was purely literary, philosophical, and ethical in character. There was little that could be called concrete or practical in the modern sense of the word, neither was there anything requiring the knowledge of the experimental method or of inductive reasoning. Education strongly resembled the form of training which prevailed in Europe for two centuries after the revival of Greek learning. This peculiar quality of Chinese education produced a prodigious effect on the career of the nation. It accounts for the present comparatively backward condition of China, explaining why the country made little progress in the arts of modern life and in the modern sciences until the last decade. Since her contact with the western nations, her educational system has undergone a radical change through the introduction of modern subjects of study and the education of many of her students in foreign lands. The effect of this change upon her national life has been marvelous. It set the country on the high road of progress and reform. A great revolution, at once political, industrial, and social, is taking place under our very eyes. Educational reform in China now forms the very pivot around which all other reforms

---

[1] Cf. Eliot, Charles W., The Concrete and Practical in Modern Education, pp. 1-7.

turn, for it is to education that China is looking for the men to steer the ship of state into the haven of safety. This close relationship between education and national progress should be an argument for the introduction of a more practical training in the public schools of China.

Education and Government Service

As in the West education was at one time regarded as a preparation only for the ministry, for medicine, and for law, so in China education was regarded for many centuries as a preparation not for practical, every-day life, but for the narrow official career. The highest ideal that parents used to hold up to their sons was official life. This ideal so dominated the Chinese mind that industrial pursuits came to be looked upon with disdain, as unworthy of a scholar. Even now many graduates of modern schools consider government position as the legitimate reward of their schooling. This partly accounts for the fact that schools of political science existing in large numbers are often filled to overflowing, while industrial schools find difficulty in securing a sufficient number of students. The mistake of making education merely a means of training for official life is one which China cannot afford to repeat under the new educational system. The experience of India in this matter should be a warning to China. In the former country a large number of young men are educated to pass the civil service examinations, with the result that the supply is in excess of the demand. The political agitators in India are found among this class which education has rendered unfit for anything except employment in the government. This conception of education as preparation for official life, though it is gradually passing away, must be quickly and entirely taken out of the constitution of the Chinese mind and be replaced by the broader conception which regards education not only as a preparation for government service, but also as a means for training men for all phases of life. The sooner this is done, the better it will be for China.

Centralization Versus Decentralization

The question as to what kind of educational administrative system China should aim to develop is no less serious. The and sectional feeling and substituting in its place a national consciousness, the need for a national language instead of the present babel of tongues, the importance of having common national ideals and habits of disciplined obedience to law and authority, all seem to call for a centralized system of administration. On the other hand, the extent of the territory, the necessity of adapting education to local needs, and the desirability of providing opportunity for local initiative and for the participation of the various social organizations in the administration of education, all demand that a decentralized system of education be developed. Although the advantages of one system often prove to be the disadvantages of the other, it is nevertheless not impossible to secure such a blending of the two that the benefits of both may be retained without sacrificing the important advantages of either. The system now in vogue in China seems to be tending in this direction. The Ministry of Education prescribes a general course of study for the nation as a whole, but certain changes are allowed in order to adapt it to local needs. Books written by individuals for use as text-books in schools require the approval of the Ministry of Education, but each province has a text-book commission charged with the duty of selecting, among the list of certified books, those suitable to the needs of the province. These and other arrangements all reveal the fact that while uniformity is sought for, sufficient room is left for the exercise of local initiative. This tendency to avoid the dangers of the two extremes is, on the whole, a wise one, and should be even more carefully worked out.

The policy introduced after the establishment of the republic, of having the central government responsible for the maintenance of higher education, the provincial government for secondary education, and the local government for all forms of primary education, is also an excellent feature of the present administrative system, for it places a definite responsibility upon a definite authority and does away with all conflicts of interest, as well as the shirking of responsibility in the administration of education.

Curriculum

The elimination of the classics as a regular subject of study, the reduction of the over-crowded curriculum, and the introduction of more modern subjects of study are steps in the right direction to make the curriculum what it should be. For further improvement the following suggestion may be made: a smaller proportion of the average school time should be given to memory studies, e. g., language and the like, and a larger proportion to scientific studies, to the domestic arts, to music and drawing, and in general to the acquisition of skills. The teaching of Mandarin should be widely introduced, in spite of the difficulties involved, in order to hasten the unification of the spoken language of China.

In the eagerness to learn from the West there is a danger of over-emphasizing the importance of western education at the expense of all that is really vital in the Chinese national life. This danger should by all means be carefully guarded against. For to give the Chinese an education only along lines laid down as the best for men in the West would not guarantee the drawing out of the best for the Chinese. There must be a commingling of the best the West has to offer with that which has been proved unquestionably best for China through the centuries of her wonderful history Dr. Paul Monroe, in his address before the Kiangsu Edueational Association, struck the same keynote when he said: "The task before the Chinese educators is to preserve the best—the essential, not the detail—of their old culture, and to add to it the essential—not the detail—of western culture. It should be a fusion, not a substitution, and a fusion not too rapidly or too radically undertaken.[2]

In connection with the question of selecting materials for the curriculum, there is a demand for a wider introduction of hand-work, eye-work, and sense-training into the schools. The new generation should be given every chance to become acquainted with the concrete and the practical, and to gain a knowledge of experimental method and inductive reasoning, for it is undoubtedly true that most of the occidental progress in the arts and sciences, in morality, and in manufactures, transportation, finance, commerce, and trade has been accomplished within the last century by the use of the inductive method of accurate observation, exact record, and limited inference.[3] At all hazards, the rising generation of China must be given a training in elementary science, in exact observation and faith-

---

[2] *Chinese Students' Monthly*, December, 1913, p. 129.
[3] Cf. Eliot, Charles W., Some Roads towards Peace, pp. 5-6.

ful record, for upon this training depends largely the ultimate success of the new republic. The practice existing in Chinese schools, of having groups of teachers and pupils take occasional "walks" into the country is an excellent feature of the new school system and should be fully utilized, for on these walks there is an opportunity to teach the children to observe closely and accurately, and to study the actual natural objects and not pictures only or, worse still, mere descriptions.

Method of Education

Professedly China has done away with the traditional method of education which places a premium upon memorizing. But manifestly such a strong feature of the educational system which was in force for centuries cannot be eliminated in a brief period of time. It is not surprising, therefore, that one still finds in the schools of China too great a stress upon memorizing and too little upon active use of materials by the student. In some schools the dominant method is lecturing by the teacher, and memorizing by the student. Too often the change has been in the subjects memorized and not in the method used. So long as this procedure continues, very slight advance can be made in the mastery of western learning, whether it be language, literature, mathematics, or natural science. To remedy the evil, training in observation and the acquisition of skills, should be made to predominate over memory training. The teachers as well as the pupils in China, like those of other nations, need constantly to be reminded of the fact that while the ability to memorize is a great asset in one's education, it is after all only a means to an end, only a tool. For, to quote the words of Dr. Monroe again, "the real purpose of studying a language is to be able to use it, of studying mathematics to apply it to one's daily problems, or of studying science to be able to use the method developed in the control of natural phenomena for the service of man."[4]

One more defect in method needs to be remedied, namely, too great a stress upon the external form of things, upon the verbal phase of education. Instead of emphasizing the process or the method of science that is of great value, both the teacher

[4] *Chinese Students' Monthly*, December, 1913, p. 130.

and the pupil are often satisfied to accept the conclusions reached by others. This evil can be remedied by training teachers to teach natural and physical sciences in such a way as to strengthen the powers of observation and develop the capacity for making an exact record of the facts and then drawing the just, limited inference from the facts observed and compared. Dr. Eliot maintains that the best way to withdraw the Oriental mind in part from the region of literary imagination and speculative philosophy which is congenial to it, and to give it the means of making independent progress in the region of fact and truth, is to teach science, agriculture, trades, and economics in all Eastern schools by the experimental, laboratory method which within fifty years has come into vogue among the Western peoples.[5] Commercial, industrial, and social reform would be greatly promoted by the diffusion of such instruction among the rising generation. In his opinion, such instruction, actively carried on for fifty years throughout the Eastern world, would modify profoundly the main differences between the working of the Occidental and the Oriental mind.

Education of Women

In the earlier chapters we have observed that both the ancient and the traditional system of public education made little or no provision for the intellectual education of women, although great emphasis was placed upon their moral training. Under the new system the education of women is receiving greater and greater emphasis. The provisions made one after another for primary, normal, and middle schools for girls, the facts that the government intends soon to establish two higher normal schools for women and that there are in China to-day scores of girls' normal schools, all go to show that Chinese opinion in regard to the education of women has been so liberal and so well carried into effect that a new status of women is beginning to develop in China. It will not be long before special provision for women's colleges must be made in order to meet the demand for higher education. That Chinese women, like their sisters in other nations, will soon take a more prominent part in public life is inevitable.

---

[5] Cf. Eliot, Charles F., Some Roads towards Peace, p. 56.

Training of Teachers

The ample provision for making a proper normal training financially possible to students by remitting the tuition fees and by defraying their living expenses while at school is one of the best phases of the present system of Chinese education. This provision which ensures a large number of normal school graduates for the teaching service, together with the proposed adoption of a system of pensions for teachers and a standard scale of teachers' salaries, should be sufficient inducements not only to keep a larger number of teachers in service, but also to enlist those of better education, such as returned students and the like, in the teaching ranks.

The great need in China to-day is for more and better normal schools of the higher type to train teachers for secondary schools. At present such schools are few in number and their work falls below the desired standard. The fact that the government intends to establish in the near future six higher normal schools for men and two for women is a clear indication that it is coming to appreciate the importance of secondary education and to realize that professional training for teachers underlies the success of any educational scheme.

The emphasis that is being placed upon the education of women and the fact that women in China are taking a more prominent part in public life indicate that the time is approaching when most of the primary school positions will be filled by women, as is the case in some of the modern nations. This reminds one of the great need for more girls' normal schools, which are fewer by far than those for boys. At present the percentage of women in the total number of those who are teaching in the modern schools is not available, but it is generally known to be very small. This is due to two reasons: first, the social condition in China has not been favorable to the employment of women in public schools, except in those established exclusively for girls; and second, the number of women who are competent to teach is much smaller than that of men owing to the fact already suggested that while the education of boys has always been encouraged in China, the general popularity of education for women is comparatively recent. Indeed, women teachers have been so scarce that there were not even enough to supply the demand of the girls' schools. To be sure, it is not difficult to find women to give instruction in embroidery, Chinese language, and the like, but women who are competent to teach the other subjects of the modern curriculum have been very rare. Under such circumstances the employment of men teachers, foreign women, and those who had taken short courses in normal schools became necessary.

The present condition in China demands that much more should be accomplished in the direction of improving the knowledge and efficiency of those in the teaching service. Agencies for that purpose, such as teachers' institutes, summer schools, extension teaching, correspondence study, local teachers' meetings and conferences, teachers' associations, and reading circles, so frequently found in Western countries, are still sadly wanting in China, although a good beginning has already been made in this direction. This insufficiency of the various forms of organized effort for aiding professional growth becomes all the more deplorable when one recalls the fact that no efficient supervisory corps has yet been developed. To remedy this state of affairs, it seems necessary for the government to offer incentives, such as subsidies and the like, for the encouragement of all effort put forth for the betterment of the teaching staff.

General Outlook

This treatment of the present educational situation in China is necessarily incomplete. Perhaps enough has been said to indicate the fact that the work of reconstruction in education, and other phases of China's national life, is already well started and started with a great determination to win. The problem of supplying educational facilities for China's millions is so gigantic in its scope and so complicated in its character that its successful solution calls for not only the highest professional skill, but a great deal of enthusiasm, patriotism, and altruism. The system existing to-day, being in its infancy, is naturally full of imperfections, especially when it is compared with the systems of other enlightened nations, which still show room for improvement in spite of decades of adjustment and toil The defects of the schools are, in the main, only those which might have been expected and were almost unavoidable in the early stages of an educational effort made on so large a scale and involving so wide a departure from previous methods. Of one thing there is not the slightest doubt namely China is now confident that given sufficient time she will be able to work out her salvation in spite of the fact that the problem is fraught with difficulties. For the present she needs time to regain her breath from the shock which she experienced in the transition from monarchy to republic. She needs time to consider what are the elements in western education best adapted to further her vital interests, and what are the elements in her own system which have proved most favorable through the centuries of her history and which should be preserved with all vigor and tenacity. In short, she needs time to readjust herself to the new conditions which now surround her.

APPENDIX

TABLE I

Curriculum of Lower Primary School

Subjects	*1st Year*	*2nd Year*	*3rd Year*	*4th Year*
Morals	2	2	2	2
Chinese language	10	12	14	14
Arithmetic	5	6	6	5
Manual work	1	1	1	1
Drawing		1	1	Boys 2 Girls 1
Singing }	4	4	1	1
Physical culture }			3	3
Sewing (girls)	..	..	1	2
Totals hours per week	22	26	Boys 28 Girls 29	Boys 28 Girls 29

TABLE II

Curriculum of Higher Primary School

Subjects	*1st Year*	*2nd Year*	*3rd Year*
Morals	2	2	2
Chinese language	10	8	8
Arithmetic	4	4	4
Chinese history }	3	3	3
Geography }			
Nature study	2	2	2
Manual work	Boys 2 Girls 1	Boys 2 Girls 1	Boys 2 Girls 1
Drawing	Boys 2 Girls 1	Boys 2 Girls 1	Boys 2 Girls 1
Singing	2	2	2
Physical culture	3	3	3
Agriculture (boys)	..	2	2
Sewing (girls)	2	4	4
English	..	..	(3)
Total hours per week	Boys 30 Girls 30	Boys 30 Girls 32	Boys 30 (33) Girls 32 (35)

TABLE III

CURRICULUM OF THE BOYS' MIDDLE SCHOOL

Subjects	*1st Year*	*2nd Year*	*3rd Year*	*4th Year*
Ethics	1	1	1	1
Chinese language	7	7	5	5
Foreign language	7	8	8	8
History	2	2	2	2
Geography	2	2	2	2
Mathematics	5	5	5	4
Nature study	3	3	2	..
Physics and chemistry	..	..	4	4
Civics and economics	..	..	..	2
Drawing	1	1	1	2
Handwork	1	1	1	1
Music	1	1	1	1
Physical culture	3	3	3	3
Total hours per week	33	34	35	35

TABLE IV

CURRICULUM OF THE GIRLS' MIDDLE SCHOOL

Subjects	*1st Year*	*2nd Year*	*3rd Year*	*4th Year*
Ethics	1	1	1	1
Chinese language	7	6	5	5
Foreign language	6	6	6	6
History	2	2	2	2
Geography	2	2	2	2
Mathematics	4	4	3	3
Nature study	3	3	2	..
Physics and chemistry	..	..	4	4
Civics and economics	..	..	..	2
Drawing	1	1	1	1
Manual work	1	1	1	1
Household arts and gardening	..	2	2	2
Sewing	2	2	2	2
Music	1	1	1	1
Physical culture	2	2	2	2
Total hours per week	32	33	34	34

TABLE V

FULL COURSE OF THE BOYS' NORMAL SCHOOL

Subjects	*Preparatory Course*	*Regular Course A* *1st Year*	*2nd Year*	*3rd Year*	*4th Year*
Ethics	2	1	1	1	1
Education	..	..	4	4	11
Chinese literature	10	5	4	3	2
Writing	2	2	1	..	..
English	4	5	5	4	3
History	..	2	2	2	..
Geography	..	2	2	2	..
Mathematics	6	4	3	2	2
Nature study	..	3	2	2	
Physics and chemistry	..	..	3	3	2
Civics and economics	..	..	..	..	2
Drawing	2	} 3 (Drawing and Manual work)	3	*4	*4
Manual work	..				
Agriculture	..	..	..	3	3
Music	2	2	1	1	1
Physical exercise	4	4	4	4	4
Total hours per week	32	33	35	35	35

*History of art 1, Manual work 3.

TABLE VI

SHORT COURSE OF THE BOYS' NORMAL SCHOOL

Subjects *Regular Course B*	*One Year*
Ethics	1
Education—history and theory 7; practice 8	15
Chinese literature	2
Mathematics	2
Nature study	} 3 (Nature study and Physics and chemistry)
Physics and chemistry	
Drawing	} 3 (Drawing and Manual work)
Manual work	
Agriculture	4
Music	2
Physical culture	3
Total hours per week	35

TABLE VII

Full Course of the Girls' Normal School

Subjects	*Preparatory Course*	*Regular Course A* 1st Year	2nd Year	3rd Year	4th Year
Ethics	2	1	1	1	1
Education	..	..	4	4	11
Chinese literature	10	6	3	3	2
Writing	2	2	1	..	..
History	..	2	2	2	..
Geography	..	2	2	2	..
Mathematics	5	3	3	2	2
Nature study	..	3	2	2	..
Physics and chemistry	..	..	2	3	3
Civics and economics	..	..	..	..	2
Drawing	2	2	2	1	1
Manual work	..	2	2	2	3
Household arts and gardening	..	..	..	3	3
Sewing	4	4	4	4	2
Music	2	2	2	1	1
Physical culture	3	3	3	3	2
English	(3)	(3)	(3)	(3)	(3)
Total hours per week	30 (33)	32 (35)	33 (36)	33 (36)	33 (36)

TABLE VIII

Short Course of the Girls' Normal School

Subjects *Regular Course B*	*One Year*
Ethics	1
Education—history and theory 7; practice 8	15
Chinese literature	3
Mathematics	2
Nature study } Physics and chemistry }	3
Drawing } Manual work }	3
Sewing	2
Music	2
Physical culture	3
Total hours per week	34

BIBLIOGRAPHY

A. Original Sources

Catalogues, reports, and periodicals of the various schools in China.

Chang Chih Tung. China's only hope. F. H. Revell Co., 1900.

Chiao Yu Tsa Ch'ih or *Educational Miscellany*. Current numbers.

Chou-li or Ceremonials of Chou: Chapters Tien-kuan, Ti-kuan, Chun-kuan, Hsia-kuan, Chiu-kuan, and Tung-kuan.

Chung Hua Chiao Yu Chieh or *Chinese Educational World*. Current numbers. Shanghai.

Educational Laws of the Manchu dynasty. Vols. 1-8. Supplement. Vols. 1-4.

Educational Laws of the Republic. 1912, 1913.

Educational Laws of Kiangsu Province. 1912.

Hsueh Pu Kuan Pao: Official bulletins of the Ministry of Education.

Kiangsu Educational Administration Monthly. 1913.

Li Chi or Book of Ceremony: Chapters Wen Wang Shih Tzu, Ming Tang Hui, Wang Chih, Chi I, Hsüeh Chi, Nei Tse.

Proceedings of the Central Educational Conference. 1912.

Report on Christian Education. World Missionary Conference, Vol. III.

Shu Ching or Book of History: Chapter Chou-kuan or Officers of Chou.

Statistical report of the Ministry of Education: 1907, 1908, 1909.

Wen Hsien T'ung K'ao: An encyclopedia by Ma-tuan-lin. Section on schools, Vols. 46-49 and Supplement; section Hsüan-chü or The choice and presentation of officers, Vols. 28-39 and Supplement.

Yung Wing. My life in China and America. H. Holt & Co. 1909.

B. Secondary Sources

Biot. Essai sur l'histoire de l'instruction publique on Chine et de la corporation des lettres. 1847.

Blakeslee, George H. China and the Far East. T. Y. Crowell & Co., 1910.

Burton, Margaret. The education of women in China. F. H. Revell Co., 1911.

Chamberlin, T. C. China's educational problem. *Independent*, September 22, 1910.

Chiao Yu Shih. History of Chinese education.

Chih Na Chiao Yu Shih Lueh. A general history of Chinese education.

China Mission Year Book. 1912 and 1913.

China Year Book. 1913.

Chinese Recorder. Current numbers. Shanghai.

Chinese Students' Monthly. Current numbers. Boston.

ELIOT, CHARLES W. Some roads towards peace. Carnegie Endowment for International Peace, Washington, D.C. 1913.

EUDO, H. Confucius and his educational ideals. In Proc. N.E.A., 1893, pp. 308-313.

FRYER, JOHN. Admission of Chinese students to American colleges. U. S. Bureau of Education, Bulletin No. 2, 1909.

Report to the regents of the University of California on the educational reform in China. *University of California Chronicle,* July, 1910.

GASCOYN-CECIL. Changing China. The Macmillan Co., 1912.

GILES, H. A. Chinese literature. New York. 1901.

GILES, H. A. Chuang Tzu: mystic, moralist, and social reformer. London. 1889.

GRAYBILL, H. B. The educational reform in China. Master's thesis. Teachers College, Columbia University. 1907.

HEADLAND, ISAAC T. Education in China. In Cyclopedia of Education, ed. by Paul Monroe. The Macmillan Co., 1911.

HO, YEN SUN. Chinese education from the western viewpoint. Rand McNally & Co., 1911.

HIPPESLEY, ALFRED E. National education in China. Health Exhibition Literature. Vol. XIX. London. 1884.

HUTCHINSON. Faber's Mind of Mencius. Shanghai. 1897.

International Review of Missions. Current numbers.

Journal of the American Asiastic Association. Current numbers. New York.

KING, H. E. The educational system of China as recently reconstructed. U. S. Bureau of Education, Bulletin, No. 15, 1911.

KUO, P. W. The effect of the revolution upon the educational system of China. *Educational Review,* May, 1913.

KUO, P. W. The training of teachers in China. Master's thesis. Teachers College, Columbia University, 1912.

LEE, TENG HWEE. The problem of new education in China. Bruges (Belgium) A. Moens-Patfoort. 1911.

LEWIS, ROBERT E. The educational conquest of the Far East. F. H. Revell Co., 1903.

MARTIN, W. A. The Chinese; their education, philosophy, and letters. Harper Brothers, 1881.

MARTIN, W. A. The lore of Cathay. F. H. Revell Co., 1901.

REINSCH, PAUL S. The intellectual and political currents in the Far East. Houghton Mifflin Co. 1911.

RENAN, ERNEST. Histoire de l'instruction publique en Chine. (In his Melanges d'histoire et de voyages.) Paris. 1898.

Report on the system of public instruction in China. U. S. Bureau of Education, Bulletin No. 1, 1877.

Republican Advocate. Current numbers. Shanghai.

ROSS, E. A. The changing Chinese. The Century Co., 1911.

WILLIAMS, SAMUEL W. The Middle Kingdom. C. Scribner's Sons. 1899.

World's Chinese Students' Journal. Current numbers. Shanghai.

INDEX

图书在版编目(CIP)数据

中国教育制度沿革史＝The Chinese system of public education：英文/郭秉文著．—北京：商务印书馆，2014
（中华现代学术名著丛书．英文本）
ISBN 978－7－100－10002－1

Ⅰ．①中…　Ⅱ．①郭…　Ⅲ．①教育制度—教育史—研究—中国—英文　Ⅳ．①G529

中国版本图书馆 CIP 数据核字(2013)第 120660 号

中华现代学术名著丛书
中国教育制度沿革史
（英文本）
郭秉文　著

商 务 印 书 馆 出 版
（北京王府井大街36号　邮政编码 100710）
商 务 印 书 馆 发 行
北 京 瑞 古 冠 中 印 刷 厂 印 刷
ISBN 978－7－100－10002－1

2014年6月第1版　　**开本 700×1000　1/16**
2014年6月北京第1次印刷　　**印张 14　插页 1**
定价：42.00 元